RESTORATION

RESTORATION

DISCOVERING BRITAIN'S HIDDEN ARCHITECTURAL TREASURES

Philip Wilkinson

Foreword by Griff Rhys Jones
Photographs by Peter Ashley

headline

First published in 2003
by HEADLINE BOOK PUBLISHING

10 9 8 7 6 5 4 3 2 1

Designed by Isobel Gillan
Photography © Peter Ashley
Colour reproduction by Spectrum Colour, Ipswich
Printed and bound in Great Britain by Butler and Tanner Ltd, Frome, Somerset

ISBN 0 7553 1251 1

HEADLINE BOOK PUBLISHING
A division of Hodder Headline
338 Euston Road
London NW1 3BH

www.headline.co.uk

By arrangement with the BBC

720.942 R

The BBC logo and 'Restoration' logo are trademarks of the British Broadcasting Corporation and are used under licence.

BBC logo © BBC 1996
Restoration logo © BBC 2003

0794818

This book is published to accompany the television series Restoration, which is produced by Endemol UK Productions, part of Endemol UK plc
Executive Producers: Nikki Cheetham and Annette Clarke
Series Editor: Simon Shaw

www.bbc.co.uk/restoration

PUBLISHER'S NOTE

The buildings featured in *Restoration* were all considered for the television series and are as close to the final list as possible. However, the nature of conservation is such that, in the time it takes to print the book, some of these buildings may have already found a saviour. We apologise for any inconsistency, but our priority is to give the buildings the attention they deserve and to hope that they all achieve a promising future by whatever means.

ACKNOWLEDGEMENTS

Endemol would like to thank Simon Shaw, Annette Clarke, Monica Patel, Susanne Curran and Sally Braithwaite.

Philip Wilkinson was educated at Oxford University and held a series of editorial posts in non-fiction publishing before becoming a full-time writer in 1989. He has written more than forty books for adults and children, mainly in the fields of history, architecture and the arts. He has written two successful television tie-ins: *The Shock of the Old* and *What the Romans Did For Us*.

Philip Wilkinson would like to thank: Elliott Cave, David Johnston, and James Wingate for technical advice, the staff of the public search room at the National Monuments Record Centre, Swindon, for library and research facilities, the team at Endemol for sharing information about the buildings, Sheila Watson for support, Emma Tait for managing the project so unflappably and Peter Ashley for his marvellous photographs and Zoë Brooks for tireless encouragement.

Peter Ashley photographs, paints and talks constantly about the things he loves in Britain. He is the photographer and writer of the Everyman Pocket Books on overlooked architecture and works extensively for major clients including English Heritage. He lives with his family in a remote gamekeeper's lodge in Northamptonshire.

Many kind people have helped me on this epic tour of Britain. I would particularly like to thank the following: Lucy Bland, Biff Raven-Hill, Rupert Farnsworth, Hazel Radclyffe Dolling, Judith Bowers, Byron Hahn, Adrian Kay, Joyce Green, Mike Catton, Neil Bonner, Dr. Peter Howard, Geoff Coxhead, Neil Summers, Bill Smith, Alan Lodge, Celia Ferguson, Sean Wood, John Smith, Philip Wilkinson, Margaret Shepherd, Richard Gregory, Simon Shaw, Isobel Gillan, Emma Tait and all at Headline.

All photographs are © Peter Ashley except:
Page 7: Stuart Wood © BBC. Page 10: Alistair Devine © BBC. Page 22 (left): Poltimore House Trust. Page 33 (right): Ron Martindale. Page 40 (left): page 42 (left): London Borough of Enfield. Page 94 (left): Crown Copyright. NMR. (Bank Hall). Page 114 (right): Gateshead Council. Page 140 (left): Carmarthenshire County Council. Page 152 (left): The Scotsman. Page 161 (top): Helen P Johnson. Page 172 (left): Strathclyde University. Page 176: Royal Commission on the Ancient and Historical Monuments of Scotland. Page 194 (right): Sions Mills Preservations Trust.

CONTENTS

Foreword *by Griff Rhys Jones*

Could there be any more dangerous pleasure than breaking into derelict buildings? During the filming of *Restoration*, I wondered whether we should begin the programme, 'Welcome dereliction fans, everywhere.' There are plenty of us. God forbid that I should encourage anyone. (I am not encouraging you, it's dangerous.) But I can recall when I was a kid, the thrill of mooching around that old farm building, looking for the loose door to squeeze through. Hem, hem. Usually, we had to content ourselves with peering in and guessing what it must be like, beyond the broken floorboards round that gloomy corridor corner.

So you can't imagine what a guilty delight it has been making this programme. It has got me, perfectly legally, into broken chapels and crumbling factories. Taken me, by official diktat, into the courtyards of secret, folly castles. Shown me up staircases, to the balconies of forgotten music halls. People have unlocked doors to let me rifle through cardboard boxes of shrouds (left undisturbed since the coffin factory closed); ushered me up the steps of a forbidden dilapidated Palladian masterpiece; shown me magnificent brick basement underground warrens in a fort in Essex; lifted me up to the top of a windmill; ferried me across Scottish waters to an abandoned palace of the islands. In all, we clambered or climbed in to thirty separate buildings at risk.

It has been quite a privilege to be able to visit all these places, if one tinged with sorrow and, occasionally, anger. Sorrow because I can honestly say that of the thirty candidates, the buildings you can vote for, the restoration hopefuls that we visited, there was not a single one that failed to utterly get me. Candidly, I had hardly expected it. Television, to be frank, can be a little prone to exaggeration. But Ptolemy Dean and Marianne Sühr weren't putting it on, and neither was I. There was not one place that we visited that disappointed us. I only hope we did justice to them all. The fourteenth century red brick tower in King's Lynn: superb and truly beautiful. The lino factory in Kirkcaldy: as handsome and stalwart an adornment to that town as you could hope for. The run-down country house near Exeter: a palpable, extraordinary, resonant part of our country's history. I mean it. Foolishly, I asked myself at one point, did I really believe that an old POW camp in County Durham was a worthy candidate? Surely it was high time these temporary expediencies from a period of national emergency fifty years ago were pulled down and the land

Griff Rhys Jones photographed at Poltimore House in Devon, during the filming of Restoration.

given back to the rabbits. But when we walked in amongst the ranks of huts on that hill side, and felt the atmosphere of the place, I was utterly taken with it.

I interviewed the architectural historian Giles Worsley and asked him what criteria he would give people. How should they select a winning building? I imagined that he might mention the architectural features, the historical importance, the future use, but, rather touchingly, he raised a hand to his breast pocket and said, 'It's in here. It's a feeling. If you have that feeling about a place, if it gets you, then that's the one you should support.' In the end, I was glad that I wasn't allowed to vote. I had that feeling about all these places. I wanted to see them all restored and I wasn't alone in this.

One of my jobs was to interview the supporters of these buildings. On screen, these interviews had to become a few brisk answers to my fumbling enquiries. (We had to demonstrate the dedication and the practicality of the action groups who wanted to see a place restored.) But off screen, sometimes we talked on for hours. Does anybody have any notion of the hundreds of people out there who have taken buildings into their care? I met people who have dedicated their lives to trying to raise money to save parts of our heritage. One who first saw a building as an architectural student and now vowed he would see the job done before he retired. Another who told me how she had sat down and wept, when the years spent processing forms and mustering support had finally resulted in a grant from the Heritage Lottery Fund. I met people whose work on a project had changed their job descriptions, others who spent their weekends tidying the gardens, or organizing tours, or filling in forms, or mending what remained of the roof. And since all of these buildings had to meet the rigid criterion of being accessible to the public, they were doing it for us.

And that's where the anger comes in. Because people in this country do care about their historical heritage. They feel impotent about the changes that have been made to their environment. It is not the ordinary people of Britain who have marched through our towns and cities, laying waste the proud Victorian centres in the name of progress. It is not the ordinary people who have let magnificent structures fall into decay or made countless planning applications to wear down opposition. It is not the ordinary people who have made vast social architectural experiments or pulled down entire Georgian cities for short term economic gain. It is certainly not the ordinary people who want to see a huge sprawling suburb spreading from London to Cambridge, because of an out of date report and a weak understanding of the real housing requirements of this country.

Again and again, we met people who told us the same things. Preserving old buildings makes sound economic sense. Not just because businesses like to locate to dignified organic environments and distinguished buildings, but because people do. So many of the buildings we saw in Restoration were exemplary products of the imagination and skills of their time. The tower house in Cumbria (what a thing to make and design this strange fortified house!). The swimming baths in Manchester, built with such care and attention, because baths were a new idea and Manchester was rich and wanted to show off. These were and always will be magnificent structures in themselves. Add to that the lustre of their histories, and the interest they excite in the most casual visitor, and you have magical places: nodes of achievements, lodestones of fascination. You can't just casually cast away these treasures.

Oh calm down. It's only a game, and, surely, there's only one winner. Everybody has said to me, 'So, what happens to the others, then? You bulldoze them do you?' For three years I worked on a campaign to raise money for the Hackney Empire in the East End and I know that publicity is certainly the oxygen of restoration. There will only be one winner, but all the buildings that feature in Restoration will get exposure, and I am confident that after seeing them on television and reading about them here, people will get out there and help. It's that help that will make the difference.

It is the ones that were not on *Restoration* and are not in this book that I worry about. There are thousands of buildings at risk in this country. That means buildings of historic or architectural interest, lovely buildings, buildings that look good and feel right which are in danger of imminent destruction. I had to travel around the entire country to make this programme and I stayed in a lot of Britain's big towns. They are shocking. Believe me, too many of our great cities have been ripped apart and desecrated, for what? Parking lots, pedestrianized spaces where no sane pedestrian would walk and concrete blanks. We haven't got so much we can afford to let it go. We should all look out for those never to be repeated handsome old buildings and give them our support. I hope *Restoration* has been a tonic to the crumblies. Certainly this book will help us all to see what glorious things some of these old wrecks really are. There's life in them yet. Let's get restoring.

GRIFF RHYS JONES *May 2003*

Introduction

Marianne Sühr trained as a building surveyor and has a special interest in the construction and repair of old buildings. She organizes events and teaches building conservation, and has a range of practical experience in crafts such as mud masonry and stone conservation. She is currently restoring an eighteenth-century farmhouse.

Ptolemy Dean is an architect who has worked on the conservation of a number of Grade I listed buildings. He has made a special study of the architect Sir John Soane and has been responsible for the Millennium Project to repair, clean, and floodlight Southwark Cathedral. He is currently involved in several projects for the improvement of country houses and their landscape settings.

OPPOSITE *As a building decays, a bewildering array of problems – such as collapsing walls, missing windows and disappearing roof coverings – can face the restorer.*

Castles and churches, houses great and small, theatres and railway stations, shops and industrial buildings – Britain is incredibly rich in buildings of all sorts. A large number of these buildings are ancient or have special architectural or historical interest. There are churches that were built before the Normans arrived in 1066 and houses hundreds of years old. Many have worn extraordinarily well. But a surprising number are in danger. In England alone, the English Heritage Buildings at Risk Register includes almost 1,400 entries. Lists maintained by other regional bodies, such as the Scottish Civic Trust and the Ulster Architectural Heritage Society, tell a similar story. And most of these buildings are known only to local people and specialists.

The BBC television series *Restoration* explores this hidden architectural heritage and offers a way forward. The programme tells the stories behind thirty buildings at risk. Two expert presenters, architect Ptolemy Dean and building surveyor Marianne Sühr, travel the country investigating them. Like architectural detectives, they explore each one, assessing its age, unpicking its development, working out how it came to be at risk, and suggesting how it might be restored. The two presenters complement each other well. Ptolemy has a special knowledge of Georgian architecture, Marianne's skill is in the history and use of traditional building materials. Both are at home in old buildings of all periods and are actively involved in restoration projects and in campaigning for old buildings. Their skill and enthusiasm make them ideal guides.

But *Restoration* goes much further than telling these thirty stories, fascinating as they are. The series offers viewers the chance to make a difference by voting for the building they believe to be most worthy of restoration. The thirty buildings have been selected from the various official lists of structures in need of restoration – English Heritage's Buildings at Risk Register and the lists maintained by the Scottish Civic Trust and the Ulster Architectural Heritage Society. Welsh buildings have been selected in consultation with Cadw, the heritage organization for Wales. Viewers will be invited to vote on three restoration candidates in each of the ten programmes. The resulting ten finalists will then go forward for a further vote to decide a winning building, for which funds will be raised for restoration. But in a sense all the buildings should be winners, because the publicity generated by the series will help their custodians put the case for funding from elsewhere.

If a building loses its roof covering the rest of the structure is immediately put at risk.

The thirty candidates range from a tiny croft to grand country houses, from theatres to factories. They are all of great interest, and they all have enthusiastic supporters who are working to preserve them. But they all need help, before it is too late to save them. In some cases, major buildings are in such poor condition that they need urgent repairs to stop them falling down. How has this happened? Every building at risk has its own story to tell. Some have been neglected for years. Others, particularly the country houses, have owners who try hard to maintain them, but lack the money and resources needed to run and repair a complex old building. Sometimes, an owner's needs change, forcing a move to a different building and leaving the old one standing empty – this has been the fate of many industrial buildings. In some cases an alternative use has been found for a redundant building, but a use that does not respect its design or fabric – a theatre used as a storage space, for example.

So dilapidation can happen in many different ways, but the results are sadly similar. Buildings stand empty, holes appear in roofs and windows, damp gets in, and a cycle of decay begins. Rot destroys the parts of the structure made of wood, frost attacks masonry and moisture rusts the ironwork. Meanwhile, vandals speed up the process of destruction, as do invasive plants, from ivy to saplings.

Numerous individuals and organizations fight this destruction, and some have been working on behalf of the built environment for over a century. The National Trust, for example, was founded in 1895 to preserve places of historic interest and natural beauty. It is a charity, independent of government, and cares for more than 200 historic houses, as well as numerous other buildings and over 600,000 acres of countryside. English Heritage, Historic Scotland and Cadw maintain many historic monuments and buildings in England, Scotland and Wales. Other bodies, such as the Churches Conservation Trust and the Landmark Trust, also do a great deal of important work restoring and caring for notable buildings and the Architectural Heritage

When saplings and bushes take root near a wall, their roots can affect foundations and bring destruction in their wake.

Birds are quick to occupy empty abandoned buildings and droppings are often the most obvious evidence of their presence.

Fund offers vital support. The Society for the Protection of Ancient Buildings advises, educates and campaigns on behalf of our architectural heritage. And much conservation work is funded and carried out by private individuals, the owners and custodians of buildings who pour millions of pounds and years of effort into their maintenance.

All this activity takes place within a framework of planning legislation that is designed to protect important historical buildings from destruction or decay. The listing system, which grades buildings of particular historic or architectural interest, highlights structures of special importance. The system is not meant to fossilize buildings – it is accepted that in order to preserve a building, alterations sometimes have to be made and new uses may have to be found. But it ensures that the architectural and historical qualities of a structure are looked at carefully before changes are made.

There is still an enormous amount to do. Hundreds of buildings are in urgent need and every one is different. Every restoration, therefore, needs to be different too, and there is a range of broad approaches. At one extreme is what might be called the 'museum approach', possible when a building is to be dismantled, re-erected, and displayed as an example of a particular building type. Faced with, say, the remains of a late medieval timber-framed hall house, a restorer might decide to take the building back, as nearly as possible, to how it might have been when it was built. This would entail removing relatively recent additions, from modern decorations to later extensions, ceilings, and floors. The timber framework would then be dismantled, re-erected on the museum site, and given new infill and roof covering. This kind of restoration has been used to great effect at collections of old buildings, such as the Weald and Downland Museum in Sussex and Worcestershire's Avoncroft Museum.

Another approach is to restore the building to the state it was in at a particular point in its history. When the great country house at Uppark, set high on the South Downs in Sussex, suffered a disastrous fire in 1989, this was the procedure adopted by its owners, the National Trust – they decided to restore the house to its condition immediately before the fire. And so the stunning house displays once more its late seventeenth-century beginnings, its beautiful eighteenth-century interiors, and nineteenth- and twentieth-century modifications – even if many details actually date from the 1990s.

These methods are fine for buildings that are intended mainly for study or display. But for the vast majority of buildings at risk they may not be an option. No restoration project ends with the restoration. All buildings – especially old ones – need regular maintenance, and this is never cheap. So if a restored structure is to survive, it will need a viable use, something that will help it pay its way, while also preserving its historic fabric.

In such cases a much greater degree of compromise may be required. The restorer has to take a hard look at the building and decide which parts should be preserved, which might be renewed, and whether any elements have to be removed completely. If the structure is partly or wholly in ruins, can it be rebuilt or should the fabric be stabilized, so that it does not decay further? If the walls and structure of the building are important, but the interior was remodelled later, can the latter be sacrificed to make the building more usable?

More tough decisions need to be taken about a building's contents. They may be later than the main building, but they may still have historical importance. Sometimes the contents are just as important as the building that houses them, and often there is an intimate relationship between building and contents that must not be disturbed if the historical importance of both is to be preserved.

Some of today's best loved and most successful buildings have grown out of such difficult restoration projects. The Tate Modern, in a former power station on London's Bankside, is one of the capital's most popular galleries. It preserves the original structure's cavernous turbine hall and its dramatic exterior, combining this with new elements by architects Herzog and de Meuron. On a smaller scale, thousands of children have learned more about farming and country life on visits to farm buildings restored by the National Trust at properties such as Cambridgeshire country house Wimpole Hall. Here the Home Farm has been revived and functions as a major centre for rare animal breeds. And in many city centres, workers enjoy the environment provided by offices converted from old warehouses and factories, where big windows provide good light and generous floor areas allow flexible working spaces.

For both large and small schemes, reliable funding is vital because restoration can be costly. Materials often have to be specially made and skilled craft workers have to be brought in. Yet the benefits are beyond price. Britain has an unparalleled architectural tradition and if we preserve that tradition, generation upon generation will thank us in years to come. But the value of restoration goes far beyond this. For a start, there is an environmental benefit. We live on a group of islands where there is limited space and limited resources. It makes sense to make the best use we can of old buildings to provide the accommodation and services that we need. The proposed uses for the buildings in the *Restoration* series range from theatres and arts centres to offices and venues for meetings. Some plans involve multi-use schemes, where rents from tenants in part of the building will contribute towards the upkeep of the whole.

Restoration brings enormous educational benefits. The more we learn about old buildings, the more they illuminate the lives of the people who built them. As well as the expected country houses and places of worship, which

Urban buildings can become regular targets for fly-posters – whether or not there is already a notice board on site.

Old interiors are fragile. Damp can bring ceiling plaster away in chunks and lift fabric or paper off walls. Fittings such as panelling, balcony rails, and balusters are attractive targets for architectural robbers.

have obvious stories to tell, the *Restoration* series includes factories that were used by forgotten industries, theatres that bring to life vanished forms of entertainment, and farm buildings that evoke ways of country life that are long gone. The buildings in the series throw unexpected light on a vast range of historical periods, from the Middle Ages to the Second World War.

Then there is the knowledge restorers gain of architecture and building techniques. These structures have much to tell us about the crafts of the stone mason and metalworker, carver and carpenter, painter and plasterer. With each restoration project, this knowledge increases – and spreads as new craft workers are trained and old skills are revived.

There can also be huge local benefits when old buildings are restored. A renovated building that becomes a tourist attraction can bring money and investment into an area. Whole city districts, such as the area around Liverpool's Albert Dock, have become richer and more vibrant, largely as a result of the restoration projects carried out on their buildings. Even restored warehouses that become offices or apartments can bring much-needed investment and life into run-down areas. But in *Restoration*, public access is a key element in the proposals for all the candidates, so if and when they are restored, essential parts of our hidden heritage will be revealed.

There are social dividends too. Local people set great store by their buildings. Again and again, *Restoration* shows how it is only through the dedicated efforts of local supporters that buildings at risk have been able to survive at all. When they are restored, occupied, and fulfilling a useful role, they will become sources of immense local pride. A major restoration project can lift the spirits of an entire area and can stimulate smaller improvements and renovations in a virtuous circle. And we are all better off as a result.

THE SOUTH WEST

RESTORATION

Poltimore House EXETER
Arnos Vale Cemetery BRISTOL
Whitfield Tabernacle KINGSWOOD

'Poltimore House is in such a state of decay, but the glory of the building shines through and you can see that once it is restored it will effect the lives of all the people who live around.'

Joan Bakewell *champions*
POLTIMORE HOUSE

'Let Arnos Vale be the flagship leading forward the movement to save all the cemeteries in the country for our living and for our dead – for those who are interested in history, in sculpture, in nature and in architecture.'

Lucinda Lambton *champions*
ARNOS VALE CEMETERY

'Whitfield is one of the men who built this country. He helped persuade the working classes to take religion seriously and therefore helped to form the character of the Industrial Revolution. By saving his Tabernacle we can celebrate his memory.'

Roy Hattersley *champions*
WHITFIELD TABERNACLE

Parts of the South West seem typically English, parts like another country. Cornwall, with its rugged cliffs, crashing breakers and hidden villages down narrow lanes, has its own separate identity, its own industries, even its own language. It is one of Britain's Celtic places, sometimes as much like western France as the rest of England, with its villages named after foreign-sounding Christian saints and missionaries. The county is often bare and treeless, the rock is hard granite and the landscape is in many places scarred by the search for Cornwall's natural resources – tin, copper and china clay. The county's famous fishing villages, which become holiday villages in the summer, are like homely oases.

Further east, in Devon and Somerset, the landscape is softer and less industrial. Green pasture is home to sheep and dairy cattle. In the villages, thatch is a common roofing material, and in Somerset there are warmer-hued stones such as chert, a brownish, flint-like rock, and limestone. This is the southern end of the great belt of limestone that sweeps across England from Somerset to Yorkshire, yielding excellent building stone much of the way. As Cotswold stone, it is used in towns and villages across Gloucestershire and its neighbouring counties, to create landscapes and townscapes that are quintessentially English.

People came to the South West thousands of years ago, and traces of their buildings can still be found in parts of Devon and Cornwall. Evidence of prehistoric settlements on Dartmoor can be seen in the remains of huts, stone circles and burial places, and there are prehistoric villages and burial chambers in the far west at Land's End. These are modest sites, but since the earliest times building on a large scale took place in the South West. The great stone circles of Stonehenge and Avebury on Wiltshire's Salisbury Plain are Britain's most famous prehistoric monuments. Stonehenge, with its enormous upright sarsen stones, is world-renowned. But Avebury, where the stones encircle the entire modern village, is in its way just as impressive. These vast circles, ritual centres for millennia, are hardly buildings, but they required state-of-the-art building and engineering skills. Their creators also had the ability to transport heavy materials over long distances, for some of Stonehenge's stones came all the way from south Wales.

More recent builders, by contrast, usually turned to a local material for their houses and farm buildings. In Cornwall, this means granite for the walls and

Cornish coastal settlements are often built on the cliffs, as here at Mevagissey. Rows of houses are terraced one above the other, the older buildings nearest the harbour, the newer ones further away on the cliff tops.

slate for the roof. The combination can look rather grey and dour, but Cornish houses are often colourwashed in a range of pale tints familiar from holiday postcards. Cornwall's rugged south coast contains many settlements where such colourwashed houses stand out in front of grey cliffs, from fishing villages such as Polperro and Mevagissey to larger working towns like Porthleven.

A more malleable alternative to granite was local clay, which became a popular material for cottages and farm buildings. If there had been more trees to provide fuel for kilns, a brick industry would probably have flourished. But trees were thin on the ground, so builders used the earth unbaked, binding it together with straw and ramming it down to form walls. A wall of mud, or cob as it is called hereabouts, is hardly waterproof, so it must be set on a base of brick or stone, coated with lime plaster and given a roof with a generous overhang. If the plaster is well maintained, a cob wall can last for hundreds of years, and the pale colourwashes and often gently undulating lines of cob walls give many villages in Devon and Cornwall their special character.

There are cob cottages in parts of Somerset, too, but much of this county is in the limestone belt, as is Gloucestershire. The oolitic limestone found here is soft, easily workable, attractive and abundant. In the Cotswolds, which stretch from Bath in the south to Chipping Campden in northern Gloucestershire, it is used for everything from walls between fields to all kinds of building, and, in thin slabs forming 'stonesfield slates', for the roofs of many. Even window frames are often made of stone, especially on higher-status houses, where they can be finely carved. Cotswold villages, in which nearly every house it built completely of stone, are some of the most picturesque in England. Some, such as Bibury and Lower Slaughter, deep in folds of the hills in Gloucestershire, attract visitors from all over the world.

The limestone of the South West has a huge range of colours, giving the houses of different areas their special shades. This variety includes the white stone of Dorset's Isle of Portland, the light brown or grey palette of western Dorset and eastern Somerset, the much-admired creamy stone of Bath and the range of greys and yellows found in the Cotswolds. Such stone has always been admired, not only by visitors to the region but also by masons from all over England – Bath and Cotswold stone have been used widely, inspiring masons in centres of fashion and design such as London.

Stone was the obvious choice for larger houses, too, from the homes of medieval wool merchants in Cotswold towns such as Chipping Campden to big country houses. The South West has some notable country houses, for great families have always lived in the region, undeterred – or perhaps even encouraged – by the area's distance from London. Sir Francis Drake, for example, was a Devon man. He came from a farming family, but his success allowed him to buy Buckland Abbey, north of Plymouth, which previous owners had transformed into a comfortable country house. The South West's other outstanding houses include Cotehele, not far from Buckland Abbey. Set in a hidden wooded valley, it is one of the most charming: an intricate medieval labyrinth of small, candlelit rooms. At the other end of the scale is magnificent Jacobean Montacute, west of Yeovil, with its long gallery, decorated ceilings and stunning views.

The South West's churches are as wide ranging as its houses. Many small churches were built in a plain and simple style little influenced by big-city fashions. Cornish granite is a material that encourages a simple building style, because it is tough and punishing to the chisel, making decorative carving difficult. It is also hard to quarry, but plenty of massive lumps of the rock, known as moor stones, were lying around for the taking, and early builders used these. The tough, coarse-looking stone can still be seen in many churches in Devon and Cornwall. This grey, buff or brown material makes ruggedly individualistic buildings. And the spirit of independence established in the nineteenth century, when Nonconformity put down strong roots, meant that many dissenting chapels were built in the area. Some have been converted to houses, but others are still in use.

The main street at Lower Slaughter, Gloucestershire, follows the line of a stream in one of the valleys of the Cotswolds. Here and there, where rooms have been added in the roofs, dormer windows poke up between the limestone 'slates'.

There is a massive contrast between a Cornish church or chapel of grey, unadorned granite and one of the larger parish churches of Somerset. Inspired by the carvable quality of the local limestone and their own skill in designing tall structures, Somerset's masons of the fifteenth century produced some of the most striking church towers in Britain. In places such as Taunton and Mells, Isle Abbots and Huish Episcopi, these towers are tall and elegant. Carved with tracery, fitted with elaborate windows and adorned with sculptures, they create buildings that are remarkable by any standards, especially when many of them occur in small villages where a big church comes as a surprise. The Somerset towers owe their existence to a combination of factors – good stone, skilful masons, a community made prosperous through the wool trade, and a belief that it was worth putting up such extravagant structures dedicated to the glory of God.

The vast cathedrals of the region were also great works of the mason's art. Salisbury, famous for its graceful spire, and Wells, with its statue-studded west front, are the two best known. Exeter and Gloucester Cathedrals are also outstanding. At Salisbury, high up in the tower, is the ancient wooden mechanical hoist that the workers used to haul heavy stones hundreds of feet above the ground. Modern visitors often marvel at how these structures were created without the aid of sophisticated machines. Here's the answer: the medieval masons *did* have their machines, for they were also the engineers and innovators of their time.

The great cathedrals form focal points to some of the country's most interesting cities. Wells still retains the atmosphere of an ancient city, with its tiny centre and medieval bishop's palace. The place feels rather cut off from the modern world. But other south-western cities are bigger and have been forging links with the outside world for much of their history. Bristol in the Middle Ages was a port only slightly less important than London. Merchant venturers from Bristol were some of the first Europeans to cross the Atlantic, and the city was well placed when trade with America began to flourish. By the Victorian era, Bristol had sprouted the docks, warehouses, shops and cemeteries of a vast, mercantile city. Gloucester, although far inland, was also a major port. Seagoing craft came up the River Severn and the Sharpness Canal to unload at Gloucester's docks, meeting barges coming south from the Midlands. Many of the Victorian warehouses survive around Gloucester's docks and their huge size gives an idea of the port's prominence. Bath, by contrast, became a pleasure

Boats moor between the recently restored warehouses of Gloucester's historic docks.

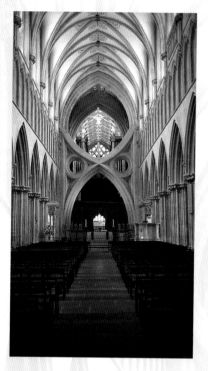

The nave of Wells cathedral has rows of pointed arches with deeply cut mouldings in the medieval Gothic style.

town, a resort to which the eighteenth- and nineteenth-century middle classes flocked to enjoy themselves and drink the therapeutic waters. A city as fashion statement, its sweeping terraces and crescents remain, their limestone forms inspiring to visitors, architects and town planners to this day.

The limestone buildings – even the industrial ones – of Somerset and Gloucestershire seem to blend with the landscape. In the Cotswolds, for example, there was a thriving cloth industry in the late Middle Ages. Every stream had its mill for fulling, and small towns like Bath's neighbour Bradford-on-Avon or Nailsworth, set in a deep Gloucestershire valley, were full of factories for cloth or other industries. Many of these buildings survive, restored and converted to apartments, offices or industrial units. They are often quite large, but they are not oppressive because they are built of the local honey-coloured stone that glows bright in the sunshine.

In Cornwall it is a different story. Central Cornish towns such as Camborne and Redruth were at the heart of the old tin-mining industry. In the countryside around them, the high engine houses of the tin mines can still be seen, their tall tapering chimneys poking up in striking contrast to the green fields around them. Many survive in ruins, years after the last miners downed tools. These engine houses are a reminder that some of the greatest innovators of the Industrial Revolution were from the South West. In the early eighteenth century, Dartmouth blacksmith Thomas Newcomen was one of the pioneers of the steam engine, building huge steam-powered pumps in an attempt to get the water out of flooded deep mines. In 1800, Cornishman Richard Trevithick began to build high-pressure steam engines, swiftly following them with the first steam locomotive to run on tracks and the first steam threshing machine. These innovations were refined by later engineers, but they started here, in the rugged, rural landscape of the far South West.

Bristol is closely associated with another of the great engineers, Isambard Kingdom Brunel. Brunel's Great Western Railway, built in the 1830s, went from London to Bristol, and, in 1838, his paddle-steamer the *Great Western* sailed from Bristol to New York in record time. Brunel's GWR station, now the British Empire and Commonwealth Museum, can still be seen, with its large, arching iron and glass train shed. The engineer also gave the city its most famous monument, the magnificent suspension bridge across the Avon Gorge at Clifton.

So the South West has a history of matching the traditional beauty of its architecture with innovation in both town and country. How appropriate that the region should continue this tendency with Britain's most famous new building. The Eden Project's enormous domed greenhouses are like nothing else, a brilliant application of engineering to create a series of entire environments. The project is bringing new growth to the surrounding area, and new hope, too.

Poltimore House EXETER

A home with a hidden history

ABOVE LEFT *At the beginning of the twentieth century, Poltimore House was finely furnished and the area in front of the stairs was an inviting reception room.*

ABOVE RIGHT *Classical columns support beams covered in ornate plasterwork, one of the highlights of Poltimore's interior decoration.*

OPPOSITE *In the courtyard at Poltimore the staircase turret is a close neighbour to a cluster of Jacobean gables.*

It looks simple and straightforward. With its white walls and rows of sash windows, Poltimore House, near Exeter in Devon, seems to be a classical eighteenth-century building – a grand house in a parkland setting, as Ptolemy observes. As they approached across the deer park, visitors from Exeter would see the south front of the house and imagine the elegant, eighteenth-century rooms behind, the perfect setting for the Bamfields, the influential local family who lived here. But walk around to the back of the house and it gets more complicated – eighteenth-century symmetry gives way to a trio of seventeenth-century gables. Within is a chaotic courtyard with narrow, constricted spaces and Jacobean mullioned windows pointing this way and that. Clearly, this is a house with a story to tell.

The story began in the late sixteenth century, when a house was built for Richard Bampfylde. By this time in the evolution of English houses, comfort and convenience were the keynotes. Big, single-room hall houses, thick with smoke from a central hearth, were a thing of the past, and Poltimore had a ground-floor hall with smaller rooms above. At the back of the present building, in the north and east ranges, parts of this early house still survive.

In the late seventeenth century the house was improved by Sir Coplestone Bamfield, a strong supporter of the king who was made Sheriff of Devon. He added a fine octagonal staircase and fitted new chimneypieces and panelling in the principal rooms. The staircase in its turret is one of the star features of

The Bamfields enjoyed fine views across the park through the sash windows of their main rooms.

Light through the broken windows illuminates the carved handrail and turned finials of the staircase.

the courtyard, with its fine timber-mullioned windows. A close look inside shows that it was built after the rooms it serves because many of the floor levels had to be raised to install the landings. The staircase and other improvements made the house a fitting setting for an owner who had a special standing in the county.

But these were nothing compared with the changes that came in the early eighteenth century. The second Sir Coplestone, another keen supporter of the Stuart monarchs, transformed the house giving it the broad classical south front that we see today. This is longer than the sixteenth- and seventeenth-century buildings behind it, making Poltimore look like a totally new house from the south. And behind this front were stunning new rooms. Some, like the Tudor dining room, were revamped, the old walls plastered over to take new decoration. In the dilapidated interior today, much of the eighteenth-century work has been ripped away to reveal the lines of the large Tudor fireplace and the interlaced pattern – known as strapwork – on the wall above.

More magnificent still is the saloon, a large drawing room decorated with plastered walls and ceiling in the rococo style fashionable in the 1720s and 1730s. This was a light, flowing style, imported from France, with flowers, foliage, fruit and seashells the favourite decorative motifs. At Poltimore, though, the plasterwork was more than just pretty decoration. At the centre of the ceiling is a roundel depicting Queen Anne surrounded by laurel leaves and lit by the rays of the sun. By putting the late queen in his ceiling, it is thought that Sir Coplestone was showing his support for the Stuart rulers – and, by implication, his disapproval of the Hanoverians, Britain's German ruling family who had occupied the throne since the arrival of George I in 1714. This was underlined by two further heads, since detached from the surrounding plasterwork: Anne's consort, George, Prince of Denmark, and William, Duke of Gloucester, the queen's son, who died young, leaving her without an heir. This stunning plasterwork is unique – there is nothing else like it in the house, and it is thought to be a one-off commission from a talented artist. It was originally gilded, as Marianne discovered as she scraped away a layer of modern paint, and some of the gold remains. It would have glittered magically in the candlelight.

The nineteenth century brought further changes, including a new staircase that juts out into the courtyard and an internal rearrangement that created two large rooms: the red drawing room and the library. A new west wing incorporating a ballroom was added in 1908. By then, the house was past its heyday. The Bamfields owned another property in Devon, and the financial strain of running two large houses was too much. So the family moved out in 1921 and Poltimore was successively a school and a nursing home. It has been vacant since the late 1980s.

To one side of the Georgian front, Poltimore's early twentieth-century west wing is on a different scale from the main house.

Poltimore's twentieth-century occupiers kept the house repaired, but at the expense of some inappropriate additions. To Ptolemy's dismay, a modern lift now thrusts its way through the main stairwell. The 1908 west wing inevitably looks like an afterthought next to the eighteenth-century south front. Modern, plastic-based paint covers the façade, holding in moisture and encouraging the stucco to peel away. These were well-intentioned attempts to maintain the house, but much worse was to come. In 1988 there was an arson attack, and since then the house has been seriously vandalized. Parts of the rococo plasterwork were stolen, as was the wrought-iron balustrade from the staircase. This was obviously removed with a sledgehammer, ruining each of the carved stone stair treads in the process. More details of carving and plasterwork disappeared.

Miraculously, some of the stolen fragments have been recovered; they were bought by a dealer who recognized their provenance and returned them to Poltimore. Among these fragments were the plaster heads of George of Denmark and William of Gloucester, which wait in storage to be restored to their rightful place.

Poltimore is a house that developed in a fascinating way. Occupied by the same family for centuries, it grew with them through 400 years. It contains many notable decorative details, from the remains of the grand staircase to the unique rococo plasterwork of the saloon. Such details may provide a fitting setting for a future use, such as a centre for the arts. Poignantly, the vandalism has revealed some of Poltimore's history, such as changes to the fireplaces and decoration, with stark clarity, suggesting how the house might shimmer in the light once more.

Arnos Vale Cemetery BRISTOL

A paradise for the dead

ABOVE LEFT *Many of Arnos Vale's tombs and headstones preserve beautiful examples of the painstaking art of the Victorian letter-cutter.*

ABOVE RIGHT *Fine carved details adorn the more elaborate tombs, but in many cases their survival is threatened by cracking.*

OPPOSITE *Encroaching saplings and weeds take root among the crosses and scroll-topped headstones – the greenery looks romantic but causes destruction.*

We take cemeteries for granted today. But until the nineteenth century most people were buried in the small graveyard that surrounded their local church. By the late eighteenth century, though, the Industrial Revolution was taking hold. People were flocking to the cities to work in the new factories and the population was rising rapidly. By the 1830s there was pressure on town churchyards and something needed to be done.

In Bristol, as in other major cities, private enterprise provided a solution, and a joint stock company was formed to create Arnos Vale Cemetery on the Bath Road, away from the centre of the city. Laid out between 1836 and 1840, it was one of the earliest of these private, out-of-town cemeteries, and it is as important to Bristol as London's famous old cemeteries such as Highgate and Kensal Green. It played a special role in the lives and deaths of many Bristol families and preserves buildings and memorials of unique quality.

What is the right style to use to commemorate the dead? The cemetery's builders rejected the idea that the place should try to imitate in some way a traditional parish churchyard. Their architect, a local man called Charles Underwood, was an enthusiast for the classical revival that was taking place in architecture and the decorative arts, so he created an Arcadian paradise with trees, long vistas and buildings in the style of ancient Athens or Rome. As Ptolemy puts it, he tried to re-create some of the romance and beauty of the ancient world.

The tomb of Rammohun Roy is one of the most beautiful in the cemetery. With its slender columns supporting a heavy stone roof, it is a delicate structure that needs careful maintenance.

Underwood had three ancient Greek styles, or orders, to choose from in designing his cemetery buildings: Doric, Ionic and Corinthian. For the entrance lodges, which look like two small temples flanking the main gates, he chose Doric, the plainest of the orders. With its columns topped with simple square capitals, the Doric order is sober and masculine. It seems to set a solemn tone as one enters the cemetery.

Between the twin lodges are wrought-iron gates. They are painted black now, but where the paint is peeling there are traces of green showing beneath. This was a colour, sometimes called 'invisible green', that was popular for park gates in the nineteenth century because it made the ironwork disappear into the landscape beyond. A more sombre colour was applied after the death of Prince Albert, in 1861, but this was not black. Truly black paint was not widely available at that time, so the Victorians probably applied a dark grey. The gates are beautifully engineered. They slide on runners through the piers on either side, aligning perfectly with the other iron railings when they are fully open. Original details, such as the kneeler stone to stop the wheels of hearses fouling the piers, are still in position.

Inside the cemetery are two other notable classical buildings: mortuary chapels for Anglicans and Nonconformists. The Nonconformist chapel is in the Ionic order, slightly more ornate than the Doric of the lodges, with its spiral capitals and rather slimmer columns. It fits beautifully into the Arcadian landscape of the cemetery, although now its elegance is offset by the stark modern crematorium, with its ugly rendered pillars.

The Anglican chapel is more elegant still. It is in the Corinthian order, which is decorative and feminine, with capitals finely carved with acanthus leaves. Above the entrance is a slender openwork tower, which, like the decorative Corinthian capitals, seems to mark the chapel out as the most important here – the building that belongs to the established Church.

Set within the walkways and groves of Arnos Vale, these buildings provide a series of focal points for an ideal, Arcadian landscape, terraced up the rising ground. The planting was done with special care, with species chosen specially to fit the classical setting and to make the cemetery a tranquil and beautiful place in which to be laid to rest.

Although the people of Bristol were slow at first to bury their dead here, by the late nineteenth century the cemetery was filling with rank upon rank of graves. From humble Gothic-style tombstones with their pointed tops to the more elaborate mausolea of the rich, they still make an evocative sight. But time has taken its toll. Through years of neglect, saplings have taken root among the graves. Ivy covers some of the stones and tree roots are pushing many of the others out of the ground. What nature has started, vandals have continued. Looking at the shattered stones, Marianne finds it hard to decide which has caused more damage: nature or vandals. Either way, the cemetery is a sad sight, especially for the many Bristolians who still visit the graves of family members here.

Perhaps the most remarkable grave at Arnos Vale belongs to Raj Rammohun Roy Bahadoor, who was born in Bengal but died in Bristol on a visit here in 1833. Rammohun Roy was a powerful social reformer in India. He was famous as an advocate of women's rights – campaigning against the custom of sati, when a widow committed suicide on her husband's funeral pyre. He was also a champion of women's education. He agitated for many other social, financial and judicial reforms, and for some he is considered the father of modern India. His tomb, designed by painter William Prinsep, is in a fitting style, with Indian columns supporting a roof with a conical spire like a Hindu temple.

In 1998 the cemetery was under threat of closure. Thanks to pressure from Bristol residents, the cemetery remained open and local volunteers took over its management. It will be a huge task to reclaim the Arcadian landscape and graves from the tree roots and acts of desecration and to restore and open the chapels and create an interpretation centre in one of the gate lodges. But doing so will restore one of the first of our great cemeteries, a place of national importance – and will give more than 150,000 deceased Bristolians the respect they deserve.

The Anglican chapel built in the Corinthian style is set at the top of a path, forming the focus of one of the cemetery's vistas.

Whitfield Tabernacle KINGSWOOD

A centre for dissenting religion

A network of rafters and purlins is all that is left of the roof at Whitfield Tabernacle.

OPPOSITE *The Tabernacle's side wall tells a tale of dilapidation – plants steadily advance up the masonry and through the windows.*

Down a side street in the Kingswood district of Bristol stands Whitfield Tabernacle. It is easy to pass it by. The building's plain, rendered walls could belong to a small factory or warehouse and most casual visitors would be surprised that it has a Grade I listing. But it has huge historical importance as one of the first centres of a religious movement that spread all over the world.

In the 1730s, Gloucester-born George Whitefield was at Pembroke College, Oxford, training to be an Anglican priest. John and Charles Wesley had already arrived in Oxford and, fired by Protestant religious ideas that had spread from Europe, they had formed a 'Holy Club' that met to pray, study the Bible and discuss theology. By the time Whitefield joined them, the group had acquired the nickname 'Methodists' because of its methodical approach to religion and Bible study.

The Wesleys and Whitefield were ordained as clergy in the Church of England, but they were not happy with every aspect of their Church. It seemed out of touch with ordinary people and sometimes with the teachings of the Bible itself. But when they began to voice these doubts in churches they were banned from preaching in Anglican pulpits, so, like evangelical guerrillas, they took to preaching in the open air. Whitefield, excluded from sites within five miles of the centre of Bristol, found himself preaching just outside the forbidden zone in Kingswood.

With his direct style of preaching, Whitefield appealed to ordinary men and women, and his sermons regularly attracted huge crowds of listeners – sometimes as many as 10,000 or 20,000. The manual workers of Kingswood flocked to hear him. Like the Wesleys, Whitefield travelled widely, preaching wherever he went. Just before he moved on from Bristol, he gave his friend and colleague John Cennick the money to build a plain and simple chapel where his followers could meet, listen to sermons and pray. Whitfield Tabernacle was begun.

The religion of Whitefield and his followers was simple and accessible. It was based on the Word of God – bible readings, simple hymns and charismatic sermons were the order of the day. The church they built was rather similar – a simple, box-like building with very little in the way of decoration. Holiness was in God's Word and in the individual's faith. Ornate decoration was not needed to express God's presence.

From the outside, the unassuming front could not be plainer. Only a few curved-topped windows flush with the walls suggest that the building dates to the early eighteenth century. It looks almost as if the original users wanted to keep a low profile. To the side, a trinity of taller windows, a large one flanked by two of a lower height, make the building look more like a chapel. But, again, there is no decoration.

Inside, the building is similarly restrained, with not even a decorative cornice where the walls join the ceiling. Tall, slender columns run the height of the building, supporting the galleries and the roof timbers. The sober, early eighteenth-century panelling on the gallery fronts remains and enough of the galleries are intact to show that they were built straight in front of the windows. 'Correct' architecture was not a priority here.

The Tabernacle's roof covering has nearly all gone, but the walls are solid enough. Where the plaster has come off, the walling material can be seen. Although bricks were the fashionable material of the eighteenth century, the walls of the Tabernacle are made of a cheaper material known as rubble stone, which was often simply scavenged from the leftovers of the quarrying process or even from river beds. It is of random sizes and shapes, and early masons stuck it together with lime mortar to make a solid, cheap and rather rustic-looking wall. But covered with roughcast render on the outside and plaster within, it was as good as any other masonry. The roof would have been simple, too. Pantiles, fired in local kilns, would have protected the fabric from the wind and weather. The Nonconformists, ever aware of the need to move on, perhaps looked on the Tabernacle as a temporary building,

Almost hidden by surrounding trees, the Tabernacle remains a resolutely low-key building. Whitfield and his colleagues were never concerned with making an outward show.

ABOVE LEFT *Before it became derelict, the chapel's plain windows were filled with clear glass, to let plenty of light into the interior.*

ABOVE RIGHT *The walls show signs of water damage where downpipes have been removed.*

designed to last only until they were forced further out of town. If this was the case, inexpensive materials were the still more obvious choice.

Buildings like Whitfield Tabernacle are sometimes referred to as 'preaching boxes': simple, square structures with lots of seats. The main priority was to accommodate as many people as possible and to seat them near the preacher, so they could hear his words. As Ptolemy suggests, God is in the Word here, not in the architecture. There is no hierarchy, no special private pews for the rich or influential. It was a place where ordinary people could come and follow a faith that offered salvation for everyone who would believe, a religion that gave hope even to factory workers whose everyday lives were dark, dangerous and depressing.

Whitfield Tabernacle was one of the first chapels of its type to be built, but thousands followed until in some parts of Britain hardly a village lacked a chapel standing simple and proud in, usually friendly, rivalry to the nearby Anglican church. In later years, Nonconformists had more money than the pioneers in Bristol, but they kept their chapels simple in design, reminding worshippers, just as Whitefield had done, that Bible and faith in God were more important than any amount of statuary or expensive gilding.

The building is in a sad state now. Roofless, it lets in the damp, and the cycle of rot and dilapidation has set in. But with a new roof it would not be difficult to restore the building to something approaching its appearance in Whitefield's time. As Marianne points out, most of the clues, from the original windows to the eighteenth-century panelling, are there. To restore it for public use, with a meeting room and other facilities for the community, would be to re-create a significant piece of religious history.

THE SOUTH EAST

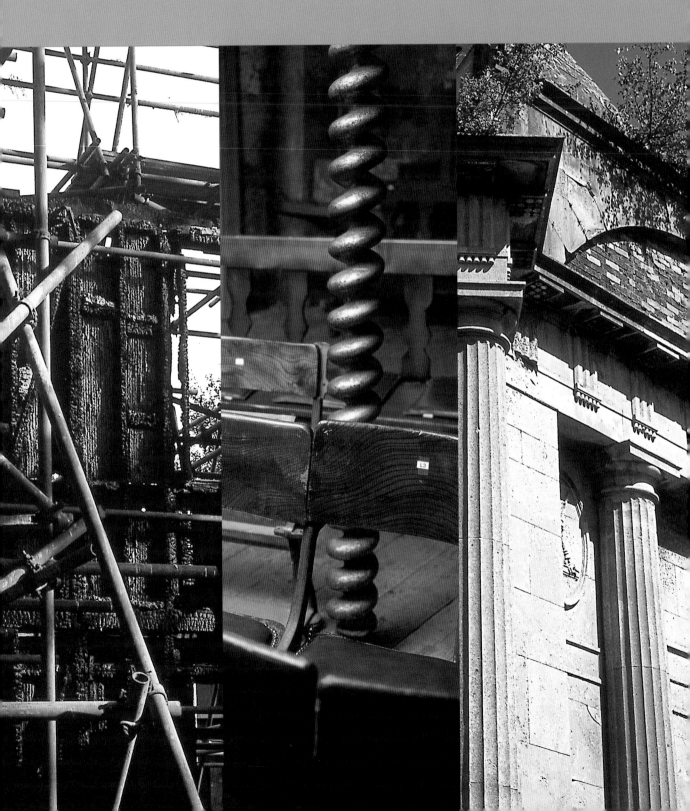

'Broomfield House has a great history and to retain its history we can't just patch it up, we need to create around it, to respect it, in order to bring it back to life again.'

Ozwald Boateng *champions* BROOMFIELD HOUSE

'Wilton's Music Hall is more than a building. It's a place where dreams were created, where people were moved and inspired. It needs people. It needs performances. The whole building is crying out for a soul again.'

Rory Bremner *champions* WILTON'S MUSIC HALL

Many visitors first glimpse Britain from the South East. If they take the cross-Channel ferry, they see the white cliffs that greeted the Roman invaders 2,000 years ago. If they fly or take Eurostar, they look out on a landscape that seems typically English, with neat fields, orchards packed with fruit trees, small towns and rolling hills.

The South East is part of the great swath of mainly low-lying country that makes up most of southern Britain and yet it is dominated by hills. The Surrey hills and the Downs skirt both the north and south of the region from Hampshire in the west to Kent in the east. Between them is the Weald, a large, low area shaped like a vast bowl, stretching across Sussex and Kent. For centuries its fertile soil has been home to orchards, market gardens and fields of hops, earning the area the nickname 'the garden of England'. Farming brought prosperity to this region early on, but another factor made the South East richer still. To the north, beyond the Surrey hills, lies London, a centre for government, business, the law, tourism and entertainment that grew over the centuries into one of the great cities of the world.

So much of the South East is prosperous, and it has been for a long time. The invading Romans made their first landfall here in the first century. The massive walls of their fort at Richborough, probably the place where they first arrived, can still be seen on the Kent coast south of Ramsgate. Nearby they set up ports such as Dover, which still has its Roman lighthouse. Such ports were built first and foremost so that the Roman army could bring in supplies, but soon they were thriving centres of trade, bringing in wealth. The Romans also built major cities, such as London, where fragments of the Roman defensive wall survive among the office blocks of the City. The invaders worked with local leaders, who adopted a Roman lifestyle and built themselves country houses, some on a vast scale. One of the greatest was the palace at Fishbourne, not far from Chichester in West Sussex. This enormous building covered some ten acres and was full of rooms decorated with coloured plaster and floored with mosaics. With their intricate patterns and images of exotic mythical beasts, the mosaics are the most beautiful parts of this lavish complex to survive. But Fishbourne Palace, although an eloquent reminder of the wealth of this region in Roman times, was a one-off. For the most part the ordinary people lived in far humbler dwellings of wood, brick and tile.

A variety of materials has been used in the houses of the South East ever since, and these houses have always revealed a range of building styles as rich and varied as the apple varieties in an old orchard. Ruddy blocks of ironstone, pale greens and glinting lumps of flint are three of the stones sometimes used hereabouts, but this is not, on the whole, good stone country. Timber, on the other hand, was plentiful, especially before the iron industry pillaged so much for charcoal burning, and for many this was the building material of choice.

One early type of timber-framed building that can still be seen in the region is the Wealden house. This has a central high hall that rises the height of two normal floors, with two-storeyed wings on either side. When Wealden houses were built in the fifteenth century, the hall formed the main living room. Open to the roof and with a hearth in the middle of the floor, it provided a generous space. One of the wings housed the kitchen and other 'service' rooms; the second wing contained private rooms for the owner. A fine Wealden house, which has been restored to its original layout, is at the Weald and Downland Museum near Chichester. In most other surviving Wealden houses a floor has been added halfway up the central hall so that the whole house has two storeys. But the original form of the house is still often visible, with its timber uprights and beams.

Daub – a mixture of clay, straw and cow dung – is the traditional material for filling the gaps between the timbers. Limewashed pale, it makes a pleasing contrast with the darker wood. Nowadays, timber-framed houses are usually black and white, but when they were built the contrast was probably more subtle, with silvery oak timbers set off against buff or yellow infill. An alternative was to fill the gaps between the timbers with bricks, sometimes laid in ornate patterns.

Daub was never completely waterproof, and heavy bricks laid between timbers could put a strain on the structure, so builders looked around for a cladding material to cover and protect these half-timbered walls. One answer came from the tile industry that was burgeoning in the late seventeenth century – fired-clay tiles that could be hung on the walls. Towns like Westerham, set among hills and woods on the Kent–Sussex border, and Burwash, north of Bexhill in East Sussex, have many houses with upper floors or even entire walls hung with rich red tiles. The overlapping tiles, sometimes curved like fish-scales, create patterns of light and shade in pink and terracotta.

In the eighteenth century, brick became the fashionable material for house-building. Many people with timber-framed houses wanted to upgrade to brick but did not have the money to rebuild. A new type of tile, the mathematical

The central section of this house in Bignor, Sussex, was probably originally a double-height space and has since been converted to two storeys. Brick, stone and wattle-and-daub have all been used to fill the gaps between the timbers.

Streets like this one in Rye are three-dimensional encyclopedias of building techniques. There are walls of brick and stone, timber-framed buildings and finishes ranging from plaster to hung tiles.

tile, was invented to solve their problem. The mathematical tile presents a flat surface to the world and when laid in courses looks just like a row of bricks – perfect for the owner who wanted to protect a timber-framed building and make it look as if it was built in fashionable brick. Mathematical tiles are still fooling visitors to Sussex towns – there are many covering houses in Brighton.

An even cheaper solution was to cover the house with wooden boards. Weatherboarding has probably been widely used for centuries, and early sawmills supplied builders with elm planks for the purpose. But in the eighteenth century, merchants began to import cheaper softwoods from northern Europe, and these made an ideal material for cladding buildings. Painted white, this cladding can be admired today in many of the towns and villages of Kent and in towns such as Rye in the far eastern corner of East Sussex. Rye is an architectural picture with one of the richest palettes in the region. Here, timber-framing, tiles and weatherboarding can all be seen side by side with the up-market Georgian brick of the rich, more fashion-conscious citizens.

Proximity to London and good agricultural land meant that some of the country's richest families made their homes in the South East. In the Middle Ages they built castles and fortified houses because the area, close to Continental Europe, was often threatened by invasion. Castles such as the one at Rochester, dominating the River Medway in Kent, show the might of the Normans. Its single great square tower, with walls up to twelve feet thick, was formidably strong. Later castles, such as Bodiam Castle north of Hastings, were built around a courtyard, with round corner towers for archers to fire at approaching enemies. But at Bodiam the main defence came from a broad moat, full of water even today.

Scores of country houses dot the landscape, with examples of virtually every style. Hever Castle, west of Tonbridge, begun in 1270, was famously the home of Henry VIII's second wife Anne Boleyn. Knole, near Sevenoaks, built around a cluster of courtyards in the sixteenth and seventeenth centuries, is England's largest private house. Uppark, north of Portsmouth at the end of the South Downs, is a gem of eighteenth-century classicism. The Royal Pavilion at Brighton is a mind-boggling collection of ironwork and onion domes, Indian on the outside and Chinese within, an extravaganza thrown together in the early nineteenth century for the Prince Regent, England's most outlandish royal. Standen, near East Grinstead, is a stunning showpiece of

Nash's fantastic 'Hindu' style Brighton Pavilion is an array of curvaceous domes, openwork screens, octagonal columns and lines of pinnacles topped with bulbous finials.

the Arts and Crafts movement of the 1890s. This is only a small selection of the dozens of interesting country houses in the region. London, too, has its outstanding houses, from the rambling brick-built palace of Hampton Court, begun in the Tudor period and extended by Sir Christopher Wren, to Lord Burlington's compact white-domed Chiswick House, the building that began the Palladian movement and brought a new classicism to British architecture.

This corner of England, so full of influential families, was also a centre for both Crown and Church. Winchester, which had been the capital of Saxon Wessex, became joint English capital under the Normans. Norman masonry can still be seen in the cathedral's transepts, and later work includes the nave, with its long rows of arches in the perpendicular Gothic style of the late fourteenth century. Canterbury, the headquarters of the Church in England, boasts the area's finest cathedral of all. After the murder of Thomas Becket in 1170, it became the country's most popular place of pilgrimage. The cathedral was extended and elaborated, and, with its soaring Gothic towers, brilliant stained glass and jewel-like shrine to the martyr Thomas, became one of the most beautiful in the land.

Meanwhile, London was expanding, too, although most of its ancient timber-framed buildings were destroyed in the great fire of 1666, so the bulk of London's architecture dates from after this time. Sir Christopher Wren wanted to rebuild London as an ideal classical city after the fire but was not given the chance because city residents and traders would not let him replan the streets. But Wren was still able to give the City of London some of its architectural glories: the rebuilt St Paul's Cathedral with its elegant dome, and the constellation of City churches around it topped with an endless variety of steeples, the myriad shapes of their pale stone towers, spires and pinnacles transforming the skyline.

After Wren's time, London grew and grew. The squares and terraces of the eighteenth century, the brick houses of the nineteenth and the garden suburbs and endless ribbon developments of the twentieth added accommodation as millions of people – from market porters to merchant bankers – flocked to the city. Whole districts, from Georgian Whitechapel and Spitalfields to Victorian Clapham and Lewisham, grew and acquired their special character. Most spectacular, though, were the entirely new types of building that appeared, mostly in Victorian times: railway termini like Paddington and St Pancras, with their cavernous iron and glass train sheds roofing the ranks of platforms; world-class museums like those in South Kensington, their façades encrusted with sculptures mirroring the exhibits within; echoing underground stations; gilded theatres and music halls. For variety and invention in building, London led the world.

London is an obvious place to look for working buildings, especially the brick-built warehouses, their walls pierced with regimented rows of windows, that serviced the once-busy docks. Many of these are now enjoying a new lease of life as offices and blocks of flats. London is still surprising visitors and residents alike with its range of interesting new buildings, too. In recent years the series of stations on the Jubilee Line extension has once more made underground travel a pleasure. Peckham's new library, a colourful building full of inviting spaces designed by Will Alsop, has made libraries exciting again and helped the regeneration of a run-down area. Mark Barfield's London Eye is perhaps everyone's favourite new structure and has won a string of architectural awards. Norman Foster's skyscraper for the Swiss Reinsurance Company promises to be the City's most dramatic office block. Its tapering shape has given it the nickname 'erotic gherkin', but the joke masks a serious purpose. The building's curved surfaces allow air to flow smoothly past it, reducing wind loads and the chill blasts of air common around straight-sided skyscrapers. Foster has brought a similar inventiveness and drama to one of London's key older buildings, the British Museum. His design for the museum's central Great Court has created one of the world's most stunning public spaces, with its vast curving glass roof and stone-clad walls. It seems to sum up London's built environment, where at every corner we find creative encounters between old and new.

Victorian engineers such as Brunel used iron and glass to make stations like Paddington the broadest structures of their time. The central aisle, shown here, is 102 feet across, and twin side aisles add a further 138 feet.

Broomfield House LONDON

A London manor house

Enfield, on the northern fringes of suburban London just within the M25, was once a country place, with its cottages, church and big house. It still has its big house, but only just. Broomfield House is now a burned-out shell in the middle of about fifty acres of parkland, a target for vandals and arsonists and propped up with scaffolding. As Ptolemy and Marianne quickly saw, it takes the concept of a 'building at risk' to the extreme. It is certainly a far cry from what the house would have been like at the start of its history nearly 500 years ago in the time of the Tudors.

In those days Broomfield was a farmhouse and, like many such buildings, was destined to be enlarged and altered many times over the centuries to come to meet the owners' demands for more space, more comfort and more fashionable decoration. To begin with, it was a moderately sized timber-framed house with two storeys. Many of its walls were made of a stout oak framework filled with wattle and daub. Over the next 200 years, the building was extended. Two new wings were added – one in the late sixteenth century, the other in the early seventeenth – to provide extra rooms, more fireplaces and greater comfort. The house now had a U-shaped plan around an open courtyard.

In the eighteenth century the building became grander still. A magnificent wooden staircase wound its way from the hall to the first floor, surrounded by murals painted by Gerard Lanscroon, a prestigious Flemish artist whose work can also be seen at Windsor Castle and Hampton Court. In the early

ABOVE LEFT *A photograph from the
1930s shows the staircase with its
painted scenes by Lanscroon.
The woodwork of the staircase, from
the twisted balusters to the carved
scrollwork, was of the highest quality.*

ABOVE RIGHT *All that remains of the
fine staircase is a few treads that stop
in mid-air.*

nineteenth century, when the house changed hands, the new owners built over the courtyard to give the house a more fashionable square plan, adding a range of Tuscan columns to make the house look grander still.

But by the end of the century, the cost of maintaining large houses like Broomfield was so high that the owners decided to sell the property, and in 1903 it was bought by the local authority for £25,000 (the equivalent to almost £1.5 million today). It became, in turn, a maternity centre and a natural-history museum. Older Enfield residents still remember the house as a place where you could see not only stuffed animals but also a glass-sided beehive, whose inhabitants transfixed children with their busy comings and goings. In the 1920s and 1930s the council gave the house a new 'face' – a black and white pattern of half-timbering recalling its Tudor origins and also reflecting the mock-Tudor houses then springing up in north London.

The fires that have ravaged Broomfield in recent years have all but destroyed the outer 'skin' of most of its rooms. This is a tragedy, because panelling, plasterwork and other decorations have disappeared. But it also presents an opportunity to look under the surface to see the building's 'skeleton'.

Looking carefully, one can make out some of the original walls of the Tudor house. Fragments of clay daub can be seen, baked hard by fire. But most noticeable is the wooden framework. The charred timbers look beyond hope, but many of the oak posts and beams are so thick that a solid core of timber remains beneath the burned outer layer, which has the texture of brittle expanded polystyrene. Some of the early walls were built of brick, which plaster and panelling would have covered before the fire. Now, long thin Tudor bricks can be seen among the debris, their coating of lime mortar still visible. They form a vital clue to piecing together the building's complex history.

Most tantalizing of all is the main staircase, which rises a few charred treads before stopping in mid-air. Yet even here there are clues that could guide a future restoration. For example, the curving shape at the bottom tread gives an indication of the elaborate eighteenth-century newel post that would have supported the bottom of the banister rail. And not far away, in storage, are more remains of this stair and the space that surrounded it – ornate oak balusters carved like twists of barley sugar. There are even fragments of plaster from the murals, odd painted hands and eyes giving hints of the mythical figures that once floated across the walls. Archival photographs add to our knowledge, showing how the fragments once fitted together to make a magical space. Such scraps bring back the world of the rich London merchant who commissioned this grand staircase in 1726 and had his artist cover the walls in glowing colours, warm flesh tones and flowing draperies.

Brickwork and charred timbers are left exposed all over the interior.

Fire can sweep through an old building like Broomfield, laying it waste in a matter of hours. Because the house has been altered so much, its walls are often a layer-cake of structural timbers, panelling and later panelling nailed on top. Between each layer is a gap through which fire can spread from one floor to another, from one room to the next. At first glance, the result seems beyond repair, a mass of burned wood and floors supported by scaffolding poles. Unlike many buildings at risk, which need a new roof here, a new wall there, Broomfield seems to need a new start, with some serious thought about how the restored building might be used.

But there is probably just enough of the structure left to make it repairable. Ptolemy believes that it might even be possible to stabilize some of the decay, allowing future users to see the level of damage and to look at some of the inner details of the building revealed by the flames. Broomfield could rise from the ashes to provide much-needed restaurant or café facilities, spaces for community use, exhibition areas and, above all, a heart for the park where it stands. It could also restore some of the local civic pride of which the house was such a focus.

Wilton's Music Hall LONDON

A palace of variety

Balconies surround the auditorium to give a large seating capacity. In Victorian times, with little thought for health and safety, proprietors used every inch of audience space.

OPPOSITE *Today this quiet alley gives little clue of the noise and bustle that must have surrounded the entrance to Wilton's Music Hall in the second half of the nineteenth century.*

You would never know it was there. Up Grace's Alley in Whitechapel, Wilton's Music Hall hides behind a façade that looks like a row of mid-nineteenth-century houses. In the Victorian period this was one of the poorest areas of London and famous for criminals like Jack the Ripper – although people were more likely to die from pneumonia or bronchitis than from violence. A red-painted door surround and the bracket of a large gas lamp are the only features that announce this incongruous building, as Marianne calls it. Inside, the contrast could not be greater. Beyond the entrance hall is a cavernous space with seats, balconies, a stage and a curved plaster roof, a music hall that was said, in Victorian times, to seat an audience of 2,000.

Wilton's now belongs to a trust and performances are staged here. But the gilded mirrors and the vast chandelier have gone and the wall plaster is falling away. And the building is so fragile that it cannot be used all the time – shows have to be timed strategically through the year so that they do not put too much strain on the fabric. Even so, Wilton's Music Hall is a unique piece of London theatrical history.

Its story began in 1850, when John Wilton took over the Prince of Denmark public house. The old pub was already licensed for entertainment, but its concert room was quite small. Wilton built on to the land at the back of the pub to create a 'giant' hall, one of a number of such large halls that flourished in the last half of the nineteenth century. Although it was altered and repaired, this is basically the building that stands today.

Wilton's was not merely large. Features such as private boxes and carpets show that the place had pretensions, too. But it was not the West End. There, the price of a drink was in addition to the admission cost and the food was up-market. In the East End you bought a 'wet ticket', which entitled you to one drink on admission. The proprietor obviously hoped that you would come back for more drinks and some of the simple food on offer.

The atmosphere at Wilton's would have been unlike the solemn silence in a modern theatre. People would have been moving around, eating, drinking and even joining in some of the songs. Meanwhile, an endless parade of acts came and went on the stage, from comic singers to operatic duets, acrobats to character singers, dancers to glee singers. Not for nothing was this sort of entertainment called 'variety'. It's thought that some of the dancers were the

first in England to do the cancan, the notorious French dance that was eventually banned because it was too risqué. All this frenetic, colourful activity was reflected in the mirrors surrounding the stage, lit by a huge chandelier that projected an atmosphere far lighter and warmer than in the homes of most of the poor who spent a few pennies on their one night out in the week.

But it was not to last. Fire and safety regulations, and a change in taste, saw the decline of variety as a style of performance. Whitechapel declined, too, becoming notorious for crime and prostitution. As a result, in 1880 the stage lights were turned down for the last time and the doors of Wilton's closed. Eight years later it was bought by the London Wesleyan Mission, which used it until 1956, keeping the building's shell as it was but removing most of the gilded mirrors, cherubs, lamps and beer advertisements that decorated the auditorium. After a period as a warehouse, the freehold changed hands until it came under the care of trust that looks after it now.

ABOVE LEFT *Stylized reliefs of fruit and foliage flank the entrance doorway.*

ABOVE CENTRE *Carton pierre details give a feeling of richness to the interior.*

ABOVE RIGHT *The glinting twisted iron columns look almost too slender to hold up the balconies.*

When its new owners first entered the building, Wilton's was a gloomy place with rain dripping through the ceiling. But they mobilized the community to give the music hall a new – if short-term – lease of life. Dozens of supporters, convinced of the value of Wilton's, rallied round. Local builders, children and business people pitched in to help. A nearby upholstery company even sacrificed a weekend to re-cover all the seats. But a lot of work remains to be done, and Wilton's feels like a building hanging in the balance.

The auditorium still has its balconies, supported on twisted cast-iron columns, its plaster ceiling and its stage. Although a lot of the decoration has

been stripped away, patches of red paint and gilding on the balcony frontages give a hint of rich colours and effects that would have surrounded the audience. Ptolemy feels that enough of these details are left to conjure up the building's original happy atmosphere. In the nineteenth century the whole interior would have been like a stage set – and one on a par with the more expensive theatres of London's West End. From a distance, the balconies look as if they are plastered, but they are in fact covered with a material called *carton pierre*. This French invention, similar to papier-mâché, is made of a mix of paper, plaster, glue and a whitener that can be made from chalk or whitewash. Stronger than papier-mâché but lighter than plaster, it could be moulded to a surface when wet. Later, extra details, such as leaf motifs, were fixed on to produce the effect of expensive moulded plasterwork.

Up above, the curved, vaulted ceiling is made of real plaster – but it is under threat. Outside, two roofs join to form a valley where water can collect. Valleys are normally lined with waterproof lead, but water can pour through any hole or crack. This has happened in many places, and the ceiling's plasterwork is breaking up like icing sugar as a result. The roof timbers may well also be affected, rotting away in the damp.

It is fascinating to find such a major survival in London's East End, an area that was heavily bombed in the Second World War and has lost many of its old buildings in the modern scramble to make every square foot of expensive land earn its keep. The building's current owners have held back the tide of decay, saving the building from disaster and earning it vital publicity. But the fabric is still fragile and only a full restoration, allowing continuous use for performances, could bring this unique building to life.

Darnley Mausoleum COBHAM

The empty tomb of a visionary earl

ABOVE LEFT *In the lower chamber of the Darnley Mausoleum, the masonry is rough and defaced but the niches still wait to receive the coffins of the family.*

ABOVE RIGHT *The top is missing from the pyramidal roof and the mausoleum is surrounded by trees.*

OPPOSITE *Plants have taken root amongst the mausoleum's masonry and are spreading along the top of the cornice.*

It is a totally unexpected building. The Darnley Mausoleum, small but very imposing, stands on a rise near Cobham in Kent, only a few miles from the urban sprawl of the Medway towns. Hemmed in by trees, it looks scarred and unloved now, but it is a powerful building, evocative of an era when the rich made their mark on the landscape – both in life and in death.

The eighteenth century was the great age of the landscape garden. The landed aristocracy were building themselves country houses in the classical style and surrounding them by acres of parkland, filled with long, sweeping lakes, curving paths and woods, all apparently natural but planted with the utmost precision to create a pleasing effect. In these gardens, small buildings, such as temples and garden pavilions, were placed at the ends of vistas and on tops of hills as 'eye-catchers'. Such eye-catchers, their white stone gleaming against a deep green background of foliage, helped to create an idealized landscape like a classical paradise or arcadia.

What better building than a mausoleum to top a rise or act as the focus of a view? With such a building, the owner could to be laid to rest in the Roman manner at the heart of his estate, bringing his memory to the mind of every visitor. This was the view of John Bligh, third Earl of Darnley. He left a substantial sum of money in his will to build a mausoleum in the parkland surrounding his family home at Cobham Hall, Kent. Darnley's will went into unusual detail about the planned building. He indicated that the mausoleum

The vaulted lower chamber is reached by a flight of steps.

should be built of stone, that it should be decorated inside with marble, and that it should have a pyramid-shaped roof. After the third earl's death in 1781, his successor approached James Wyatt, one of the most successful architects of the time, to turn the vision into reality.

Wyatt was a good choice. As a young man he had travelled in Italy and studied the classical buildings of Rome. On his return he built up a successful practice, doing all sorts of work from designing country houses to restoring cathedrals and adopting whatever style was needed, classical or gothic. He was able to produce exactly the right combination of effects required for a mausoleum – bringing a range of classical details together with elements that signalled the solemn character of the building.

The Darnley Mausoleum is certainly a solemn building. From a distance, its most obvious feature is its pyramidal roof. This is completely plain, and was an unusual feature at the time although there was one very famous ancient building with a pyramidal roof. The tomb of King Mausolus at Halicarnassus, Turkey, one of the seven wonders of the world, was topped with a pyramid and by using this design, Darnley and Wyatt may have been paying homage to Mausolus, after whom all later mausolea are named.

Beneath the roof, the details are all classical. The columns on the side walls are Doric, the plainest of the classical orders – their chaste, fluted lines lead the eye up to simple, unadorned capitals. The corners project at an angle, and have more Doric columns, and above these corner columns are stone coffins. Other decorative elements include reversed torches, emblems of

Thanatos, the death-figure of ancient Greece. There can be no doubt about the building's purpose.

Wyatt's interior was just as impressive. The basement contains rows of niches designed to accommodate the coffins of the Darnley family. On one side there is a recess reserved for the coffin of the earl himself. This basement originally had a shallow-domed ceiling, but this fell down when a gang tried to blow up the building by igniting cans of petrol on 5 November 1980.

Above this room is a chapel, topped with a dome that still survives. This is a more ornate interior, lined with pairs of columns of the Composite order, the Roman design in which the pillars are topped with capitals that contain rich decoration featuring acanthus leaves as seen on Corinthian columns and the scrolls of the Ionic order. Between the columns, the main walls follow a convex line that gives the chamber an unusual flowing form that is quite unexpected from the outside. The columns were originally richly faced with red marble, and the interior decorated with fine gilt work, but most of this opulence has disappeared.

Extraordinarily, this costly and beautiful building was never used for the purpose for which it was designed. To be used for burials, the mausoleum had to be consecrated, but the family is rumoured to have had a disagreement with the Bishop of Rochester, who was due to carry out the ceremony. So the consecration never took place, and no one could be laid to rest in the lower chamber. The Darnley Mausoleum remains a lavish, imposing, but empty tomb.

It was probably the fact that the building remained unused that led to its neglect, but worse was to come. From the 1950s onwards, the building has suffered a catalogue of abuse. Apart from the fire of 1980, parts of the fabric have been stolen, what remains has been defaced. The surrounding land has been used by joy riders who abandoned the burnt-out remains of vehicles nearby. Meanwhile, trees and shrubs have periodically taken root amongst the mausoleum's very stones. All the abuse has done surprisingly little to mar the overall effect of Darnley's building, but this solid, well built structure will decay quickly if it is not restored soon.

The mausoleum is a building that does not lend itself to adaptation or change of use. It can only ever be the eye-catcher that Darnley planned and Wyatt so triumphantly created. But it is a building of international significance, one of the best of its kind, and deserves to be conserved. This is why organisations including English Heritage and the National Trust are backing a plan for a full restoration, including improvements to the surrounding parkland, a visitor centre, and an on-site warden. Such a scheme would safeguard the building for the future, so that visitors to the Cobham area may see it once more in its former glory and remember the earl and architect who created it.

A stone coffin is placed on high at each corner of the building.

THE MIDLANDS

RESTORATION

Newman Brothers BIRMINGHAM
Arkwright's Mill CROMFORD
Bethesda Chapel STOKE-ON-TRENT

The broad sweep of land that stretches from the Welsh borders in the west to Leicestershire in the east is the heart of England. Its rural scenery embraces much that is typical of what England has to offer – the starkly beautiful peaks of Derbyshire, the gentler hills of Worcestershire and Warwickshire, the flatter lands of the east. So do its towns, from medieval settlements with streets of black and white houses still intact to Britain's second city, Birmingham, its vast growth spurred on by the rise of industry in the nineteenth century.

At the centre of the country, this area has always had a prominent part to play in history. For centuries the west was dominated by relations with the Welsh. In the eighth century Offa, ruler of the important Saxon kingdom of Mercia, built his famous dyke as a boundary with Wales. Offa's Dyke is in fact a bank and a ditch, and it originally ran along the entire Welsh border. Remains of the earthwork can be traced today, especially among the Shropshire hills around Knighton. Centuries after Offa, in the Middle Ages, towns on the western marches, such as Shrewsbury and Ludlow, were fortified to protect the borders against Welsh attack. Both of these towns have castles begun by the Normans and enlarged in later centuries. Where there was no castle, a fortified manor house was sometimes built. The best-preserved example is at Stokesay, to the north of Ludlow. It boasts a mixture of half-timbered and stone buildings including a solid stone defensive tower, a great hall also of stone, and a timber-framed gatehouse.

The Midlands have always benefited from a variety of building materials. The south-western part of the region, for example, is rich in a pinkish sandstone. Many churches in Herefordshire and Worcestershire are built in this stone, and its colour blends well with the lush green fields and the leaves of the local holly and oak trees – a landscape with a rich, evocative colour scheme all of its own. But stone was expensive to quarry and work and, as there were many trees in the south-west Midlands, most people built their houses of wood. Local carpenters excelled in the construction of wooden-framed buildings, and a child, asked to draw a 'Tudor house', usually comes up with something like the typical native building of the south-west Midlands. Villages in Herefordshire and parts of its neighbouring counties still boast whole streets of black and white houses, their timbers heavy and widely spaced, often joined together at weird angles, and their roofs low-pitched with a generous overhang. Frequently they are joined by brick houses painted

black and white to match their neighbours, an act of architectural homage that has been going on at least since the Tudor style became popular at the beginning of the twentieth century.

Further north, towards Cheshire, there is also plenty of timberwork, but in the grander houses it becomes much more showy than in the south-west Midlands. The timbers in north Midland houses, such as Little Moreton Hall, north of Stoke-on-Trent, are more closely spaced, and the carpenters developed a whole decorative vocabulary of struts, braces and beams, making triangle, zigzag, diamond and quatrefoil patterns. This took a lot of labour, a great deal of skill and plenty of timber. Walls like this were expensive to build and are permanent advertisements for the ostentation, money and status of the original owners.

But in much of the northern Midlands the local building material, pure and simple, is brick. Today, of course, brick buildings are everywhere – bricks have been popular for house-building since they became fashionable in the eighteenth century. But in many parts of the Midlands the use of brick goes back long before that. This is true in the Potteries, where one would expect baked clay to be the material of choice. But early brick houses are also present in other parts of Staffordshire, Cheshire and northern Shropshire. Early bricks were hand made in a kaleidoscope of colours – reds, purples and browns – often used together in the same wall to give a rich mottled effect that seems to alter with the varying light of the sun. This gives old Midland brick houses a feeling of liveliness totally lacking in most modern brick buildings.

The eastern Midlands boast another distinctive building style. The great limestone belt that sweeps across England passes through the Midland counties of Northamptonshire and Leicestershire. Northamptonshire especially is famous for its stone, which ranges in colour from yellows and oranges in the south to pale grey in the north. As in the Cotswolds, houses here may be built completely of local stone, with stone walls, stone 'slates' on

The neat stone cottages and church at Collyweston are typical of the Northamptonshire limestone belt. The top-quality stone for the roofs came from a famous local quarry that supplied builders far and wide.

the roof and stone frames to the windows, though in places thatch is also a popular roofing material. Smaller houses are built of coursed rubble – roughly hewn blocks of stone laid in regular layers. But in such details as the window frames, doorways and corner blocks, the masons showed their skill, because they often used beautifully finished dressed stones for these. So even an owner who could not afford a whole house built of labour-intensive dressed stone could display some stonework of fine quality. The stone villages of Northamptonshire are some of the most perfect and well built in England.

Larger houses gave the stonemasons of the Midlands the scope to do their best work, and the country houses of the eastern Midlands are among Britain's most amazing buildings. The first really big houses date from the Tudor period, when the Midlands were thriving. Most striking of all are the great houses built by courtiers and associates of Queen Elizabeth I. Three stand out and they are all fantasy creations. Burghley House, near Stamford, on the borders of Leicestershire and Cambridgeshire, was built by Elizabeth's courtier and confidant William Cecil. It is a feast of mini-domes, towers, mullioned windows and a great central spire. Wollaton Hall, near Nottingham, was the home of Elizabethan grandee Sir Francis Willoughby. It has a unique profile dominated by the huge windows of its great hall, which form a kind of enormous tower sticking up in the middle of the vast house. Hardwick Hall, between Chesterfield and Mansfield, was the home of Elizabeth Shrewsbury, 'Bess of Hardwick', the second richest woman in England after the queen. Dubbed 'Hardwick Hall, more glass than wall', its façades are nearly all windows, topped by the repeated initials of its indomitable owner, carved in stone. These extraordinary buildings, often referred to as the 'prodigy houses' of the Elizabethan period, are like nothing else in the world. They form a lavish memorial to the rich lifestyle of the Tudor court and the skill of Midland masons.

The towns of the Midlands have an attraction all their own. In places such as Ludlow, set near the Shropshire hills, the charm is obvious: the rows of half-timbered buildings, many with their upper floors jettied out so that they overhang the pavements, are an unforgettable sight. But look a little more closely, and one can see that much of the medieval street plan has been preserved, down to the narrow alleys between the shops and houses giving access to the rear. In most towns these alleys have long been built over, but here, and in one or two other Midland towns such as Tewkesbury, by the River Avon in northern Gloucestershire, they remain. Chester,

Ludlow in Shropshire still boasts some of its medieval alleys, now jammed between busy shopping streets. Victorian brick houses are squeezed in next to much earlier, timber-framed buildings.

famous for its 'rows' of timber shops and houses, Shrewsbury, with its old, narrow, timbered streets, and other western towns and cities also preserve early houses, recalling something of their medieval atmosphere.

It is an atmosphere that mirrors the Tudor period, an era summed up by Stratford-upon-Avon, the Warwickshire birthplace of William Shakespeare. The main Shakespearean houses here – the poet's birthplace and the picturesque cottage of his wife Anne Hathaway – are famous and popular with tourists. But other buildings in the town bring the era to life. The school where Shakespeare almost certainly studied is still standing, as is another less-well-known house, peaceful timber-framed Hall's Croft, home of Shakespeare's son-in-law.

There are later towns of character, too. Although people do not normally think of the Midlands as a place of eighteenth-century refinement, this is precisely the mood of Buxton, at the heart of Derbyshire's Peak District. Buxton, an elegant spa that grew in the late eighteenth century, was developed by the Duke of Devonshire, whose nearby home at Chatsworth is another of the area's great houses, this time of the late seventeenth and eighteenth centuries. Buxton soon became a rival to Bath, and one can see why. Terraces and a famous crescent of houses, built in imitation of those in Bath, typify the town's development. The bath, with its spring, and the old opera house also remain. Yet from this resort it is no distance to the mills of Derbyshire. Work and play, elegance and industry – the buildings of this corner of the Midlands seem to sum up the heritage of the entire region.

The Industrial Revolution came here early, and in part it began here. At Ironbridge on the River Severn in Shropshire in 1709, Abraham Darby was the first to use coke in iron ore smelting. Coke, far cheaper than the charcoal that had been used before, opened up the prospect of lower-cost iron, a raw material for many developing industries. Darby's blast furnace and a mass of other industrial sites (mines, foundries and factories) can be seen in and around Ironbridge. The place's most famous monument of all, the iron bridge itself, came seventy years later. Its metal arches, at once strong and delicate, still span the River Severn, a symbol of the innovative spirit that drove the Industrial Revolution in this area.

Other parts of the region are still full of buildings that testify to the burgeoning industry that followed. The Potteries, the area around Stoke-on-Trent where local clay and skill came together to create an entire ceramics industry, were once full of bottle-shaped kilns in which the wares were fired. World-famous names – such as Wedgwood, Spode and Doulton – produced their wares here, and some still do. A few early kilns survive in Potteries towns such as Stoke and Hanley to remind visitors of their story.

Birmingham, too, was built on this long industrial boom. The Soho Works, where James Watt and Matthew Boulton manufactured steam engines, is now part of a modern factory producing weighing machines. But Boulton's Soho House can still be seen. It is important not just for its links with Watt but as the meeting place of the Lunar Society, a group of scientists and industrialists who met at full moon to discuss their experiments and discoveries. Many of Birmingham's old buildings have been swept away, and the city centre is crowded with modern shops and office blocks, but whole areas speak of this industrial past. The city's jewellery quarter, many of its factories still intact, is the best known.

Until recently, this industrial past, from the coal mines of the Black Country to Birmingham's factories and Derbyshire's mills, was largely ignored by the heritage industry. Now, though, the balance is being redressed and many of these buildings are being surveyed, restored, cared for and opened to the public to give us a clear idea of the richness of the area's working history. These buildings are notable in several ways. Their construction, which often creatively used materials such as iron and steel, can be fascinating and ahead of its time. Their design can have a special beauty, especially when façades are cleaned and restored. They are associated with some of the greatest industrial pioneers, and their contents, when preserved, give unique insights into past people's working lives. The industrial buildings of the Midlands, just as much as the castles, churches and country houses, form a vital part of our history.

In 1777 the castings were made for the bridge over the River Severn at Coalbrookdale. The bridge's iron construction, and its 100-foot-long central span, made its builder, Abraham Darby III, one of the most famous of all ironmasters.

Newman Brothers BIRMINGHAM

An industrial time capsule

Heaps of cardboard boxes containing coffin furniture line the walls in the factory of Newman Brothers.

OPPOSITE *Machines, sheet metal and other equipment remain on the benches in the factory. The scene is exactly as it was when the last workers clocked out.*

They called it 'the workshop of the world'. Nineteenth-century Birmingham was full of factories producing small metal goods. Cheap jewellery, trinkets, boxes and other small personal items seemed like trivia – locals called them 'toys'. But they made the city rich. Birmingham's jewellery quarter played a key part in this business. This close-knit district received a boost in the mid-century after the gold rushes in California and New South Wales. By 1913 the area was employing some 70,000 people in the trade.

It wasn't only jewellery that was manufactured here. Newman Brothers was one of the most successful producers of coffin furniture – the range of handles, hinges, plaques and crosses without which no casket was complete. This was a high-quality industry that supplied the country's top funeral directors. Many prominent people, from Winston Churchill to Diana, Princess of Wales, went to their final resting place in a coffin adorned with furniture made by Newman's.

The business of which Newman's formed such a prominent part developed in the mid-nineteenth century when the Victorians raised mourning to a fine art. Their mourning rings and lockets, collectors' items today, contained locks of the hair of deceased loved ones, and their coffins were elaborate. Every fitting told a story. A shield-shaped plaque on a coffin indicated that the occupant was male. Down-turned torches symbolized a life extinguished. A wreath reminded mourners of the deceased's immortality. This was the tradition that Newman Brothers adopted and developed throughout the twentieth century.

The factory carried on in production until, in 1999, a change in the business forced them to close. Cheaper plastic furniture, treated to look like gold, was taking over. Few wanted Newman's costly hand-finished products. But the factory remains, a unique record of the business and its employees.

From the outside, the Newman Brothers factory looks little different from any other late-Victorian structure in the jewellery quarter, a brick building arranged around a central courtyard. In fact, its red-brick façade, with sandstone dressings, raised on a plinth of blue engineering bricks and topped with a slate roof, would not be out of place in any British city with an industrial quarter. The cast-iron-framed multi-pane windows and high entrance for carts are typical, too. What makes Newman Brothers special is the interior, which contains a virtually complete collection of the machinery, hand tools, materials and stock-in-trade of the business.

ABOVE LEFT *Open boxes of crosses and other metalwork reveal the vast range of designs created by Newmans. Whatever the style, the items were of the highest quality and beautifully finished.*

ABOVE RIGHT *Many of the items produced by Newmans were made using hand presses. The worker inserted a piece of sheet metal into the press, turned the large handle, and the machine stamped it with the design.*

Entering the building, you step into another world. The original staircase and doors are still there, as is the hand-operated hoist that serves all three floors of the factory. In the east range is the row of presses used to stamp plaques, crosses, key escutcheons and similar items. Behind them are banks of shelves that contain the die stamps used in these machines. Pieces of sheet metal lie around, conveying the impression that one could clock in, take up a sheet of metal and begin work. Near the small presses for cutting out the stamped furniture is a king-size press for the really large items some rich families required on the coffins of their deceased. Much of this machinery was powered – originally by a gas engine, later by electric motor – and some of the shafts and belts to connect the presses to the power source remain. In another area is the equipment for casting, such as crucibles for melting metal and mould which the molten metal was poured into to make crucifixes and similar items. These usually needed plating, so nearby is an electroplating shop. Here, items were attached to wires or frames and lowered into vats. They later emerged gleaming in gold or silver.

The finishing and assembling shops are on the upper floors of the building, where there is plenty of light. This was where skilled hand-engravers and burnishers put the final touches to the more elaborate products. Nearby is the polishing shop, which is partitioned off from the neighbouring parts of the factory so that the dust it created did not spread around. Yet another area contains a workshop full of sewing machines, where shrouds were made. There is also a separate area where stock was shown to prospective customers. Evocatively, a coffin stands ready so that visiting funeral directors could offer up a plaque or a handle to see what it would look like *in situ*.

And what plaques and handles they are. Many of them remain, box upon box of top-quality, hand-finished fittings, a testimony to the company's extraordinary range and to the great care they took so that loved ones could give their deceased the funeral tribute that they deserved.

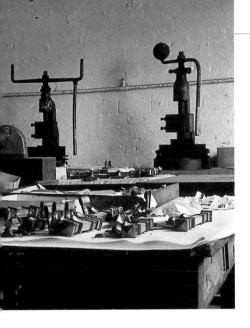

Some rooms give the impression that the staff have got up from their chairs or benches and left for a moment, shortly to return to their jobs. Hand tools, half-finished workpieces, even a worker's cardigan on the back of a chair – all seem to wait to be taken up again. For once, the overworked phrase 'time capsule' is perfectly appropriate. Dig a little deeper and still more historical treasure is uncovered. Even the original designs for many of the items survive, together with photographs of workers and of owner Horace Newman, publicity leaflets and a variety of documents – catalogues, ledgers, business accounts and shipping records. As Marianne and Ptolemy recognize, this is a priceless record, forming a unique picture of an industry.

Taken one by one, the items left behind when Newman Brothers closed its doors are unremarkable, and many of them could be picked up cheaply in junk shops or at scrap merchants. But taken together, as a complete collection, they are unique. Yet, as Ptolemy puts it, in an important way these heavy metal machines and the documents that go with them are fragile. A contractor with a fleet of skips could clear them all in a matter of days, freeing up the building for development. And old factory buildings offer plenty of scope to the developer, for anything from offices to wine bars.

Restored to its former glory, its collection conserved and catalogued, Newman Brothers could become a unique museum, perhaps with space that could be let commercially to provide income. The building's interest goes far beyond the dismal trade of the funeral director, although this has its special fascination. It creates a picture of an entire business: ironically and uniquely, it brings its history, its people, its organization and its processes alive.

A brick-built structure with metal-framed windows, Newman Brothers looks from the outside like many other factories in Birmingham's jewellery quarter.

Arkwright's Mill CROMFORD

Birthplace of a revolution

ABOVE LEFT *Amid piles of stone, work is underway on some of the buildings that make up the vast mill complex at Cromford.*

ABOVE RIGHT *Rough-hewn wooden posts hold up the ceilings inside another mill building. The lack of a fine finish shows that this was a working space, where appearance came second to efficiency and economy.*

OPPOSITE *Rather than wooden posts, metal trusses hold up the roof in this building and a variety of artefacts from its history litters the floor.*

Before the late eighteenth century, cotton was spun by hand. Working from home, people used simple spindles and spinning wheels to produce the yarn, which was then collected and taken to other home workers to be woven into cloth. This was a cottage industry. But a number of men realized that if they could mechanize spinning and weaving they would be able to make big profits.

Many of these pioneers are famous names in the history of invention, such as John Kay with his flying shuttle and James Hargreaves with his spinning jenny. But the most important of them all was Richard Arkwright, who produced the water frame, a device that used water power to spin yarn automatically. By installing rows of water frames in a mill, Arkwright created the world's first modern factory at Cromford, in the heart of rural Derbyshire. Working life had changed for good.

Today, Richard Arkwright's first mill is part of a large complex of structures: mills, warehouses, offices and even a canal to bring raw material in and take spun yarn away. The remains range from discarded bobbins, still bearing the legend 'Arkwright, Matlock', to the original mill of 1771, which is a shell, badly damaged by fire in 1929 and now bereft of its floors, ceilings and original roof. Even the window frames have gone. Inside, later structural steelwork supports floors and ceilings that do not match the window openings running

It is hard to imagine the mill floor filled with noisy machinery, all driven by the great water wheel outside. The wheel's shaft came through the round hole on the far right and a network of drive belts transferred its power to the ranks of water frames.

along the walls. Charred timbers can be found among the building rubble on the floor, and in some places the wooden lintels above the windows are damaged by fire. Signs of the mill's former glory can be seen in some features, like the imposing main doorway, topped with large well-finished blocks with a great keystone in the middle, but for better clues to what it would have been like, you have to look at the later, neighbouring mill building.

The rows of windows make the newer mill look like a typical Georgian building. Inside, the structure, too, is very much of its time, with timber floors supported by wooden posts and beams – little wonder that the fire did so much damage in the original mill. Later industrial buildings had cast-iron columns and brick-vaulted ceilings to stop fire spreading, but Arkwright's mill used ancient timber building methods to house its state-of-the-art machinery and was almost destroyed as a result.

The power source has vanished, too. A great water wheel provided the energy to drive the machinery, turning steadily until the early twentieth century. The pit where it operated, the round hole that took its shaft through the mill wall, and the aqueduct that brought the water are still in place. Ptolemy imagines the roaring and gushing of the water that once powered the machinery. It is silent now, and one object of restoration would be to rebuild and refit the wheel. Even what is left, though, tells us something about the building and its creator. The aqueduct cuts straight across the building, throwing the grand entrance into deep shadow. Clearly, Arkwright was much more concerned with function and efficiency than he was with appearance.

For a manufacturer like Arkwright, the mill offered a huge opportunity. With a water frame, one worker could produce the same amount of cotton as thousands of people could spin by hand. The potential profits were enormous, and Arkwright's business expanded rapidly. He built houses

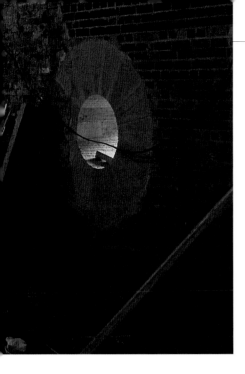

In the area around the mill there are many remains of its working past. This stone-mounted metal plate was part of the base of a crane used to load waiting canal boats.

nearby for his workers, advertised in the press and, after a slow start, whole families flocked to work here.

But although the workers were well housed, their working lives were hard. The hours were long, the conditions unpleasant and the work could be dangerous. Over sixty per cent of the workforce was made up of children between seven and twelve years old. The smallest had the most dangerous task, acting as scavengers, squeezing under the working machinery to retrieve bits of cotton that had fallen to the floor. Injuries were common, and the life expectancy of a mill worker was half that of those who worked on the land.

These people were small cogs in a huge machine. Cotton was imported via London and Liverpool and delivered on packhorses and canal barges. The material had to be cleaned before it was carded – a process that aligns all the fibres in one direction. This was originally done by hand, but Arkwright mechanized this job, too, patenting a carding machine in 1776. The carding process produced wads of cotton called rolags, and these rolags fed Arkwright's revolutionary spinning machines.

Arkwright, working with his business partners John Kay and Jedidiah Strutt, built a spinning machine that was a huge improvement on earlier inventions. In it, a system of rollers performed the functions normally carried out by the spinner's hands – drawing out the fibres into a thread and producing a controlled twist in this thread. Finally, the water frame wound the twisted thread on to bobbins. It was a continuous process and could carry on as long as the water wheel turned and the factory hand supplied the machine with rolags, changed the bobbins when they were full and joined up the thread if it broke. Unlike hand spinning, operating the machinery involved no special skills. A child could do it, and often did.

Soon there were similar mills, some of them named 'Cromford' in honour of the original, as far afield as Germany and New England. Manufacturers made their fortunes selling cheap, machine-made cotton. It was good news for mill owners, but not so good for the workers. The whole pace of working life changed. Instead of working at home, people travelled to work, and many had to move to the cities to do so. They endured poor conditions for low wages, and it took years for things to improve and for safety to become the issue it deserved to be. For good and bad, Arkwright changed the world.

The Arkwright Society has already restored some of the buildings at Cromford. Some – a restaurant and offices let out to tenants – raise money that will contribute to the restoration of the original mill to provide a unique museum and visitor attraction. When the new wheel is installed and water frames turn again, visitors will be able to see the true significance of this place of national and international importance.

Bethesda Chapel STOKE-ON-TRENT

A stronghold of dissenting religion

The windows at Bethesda are filled with both coloured and clear glass.

The pulpit, carved and panelled, is one of the most magnificent of its type remaining in Britain.

OPPOSITE *Light from the side windows picks out the mouldings on the pews, emphasizing their simple elegance.*

If you thought Methodist chapels were plain, uninteresting-looking buildings, come to Bethesda Chapel in Stoke-on-Trent. Bethesda presents a decorative face to the world, a façade of classical columns, mouldings, capitals and plasterwork that would stand out anywhere. It also has one of the most unusual interiors in a building of its type. It is clearly a special place, with a special story to tell.

Nineteenth-century Stoke and the towns around it were unlike anywhere else. Known as the Potteries, they were the centre of Britain's ceramics industry and home to famous names like Wedgwood and Minton. The townscape was populated with the unmistakable shapes of round, brick bottle kilns, belching smoke that choked the workers and blackened the brickwork of their houses. In this atmosphere, thousands worked to produce everything from drainpipes and tiles to fine bowls and vases, products that were shipped far and wide to make the Potteries famous around the world.

It was a hard-working labour force, but the area had a rough, even lawless, reputation. Drunkenness was endemic, even among children; gambling and cockfighting were common pastimes. The Anglican churches seemed unable to improve matters, and they did not appeal much to the working population. But the dissenting churches, with their more direct, down-to-earth approach to religion, made headway. Most successful was the local brand of Methodism, the Methodist New Connexion, led by Job Ridgway.

Ridgway and his colleague Job Meigh set up a branch of the New Connexion in nearby Hanley in 1797. They soon acquired a coach house in Albion Street, Stoke, and built their first church there, the ancestor of Bethesda Chapel. The Connexion quickly attracted members from all over the area, so Ridgway extended the building, then built a completely new and still larger chapel on the same site. This opened in 1820, and much of its fabric survives today. In 1859 further improvements included the addition of the elaborate façade, ready for the Annual Methodist Conference of 1860, which was held at Bethesda.

From the outside Bethesda is a building of two halves. Facing the street is the grand entrance front of 1859, with its row of Corinthian columns supporting a portico that stretches across the whole façade. Above is a whole vocabulary of classical decoration: a Venetian window, a plaque

OPPOSITE *The rear and side walls of the chapel are built in a chequerboard pattern made in bricks of two colours, a good example of a brilliant effect created with the simplest of materials.*

The steeply raked gallery seating and the tightly packed pews below provide room for a vast congregation none of whom is very far from the front of the chapel and the all-important pulpit.

announcing the building's name, a triangular pediment and lots of mouldings. Ptolemy compares this exuberant front with the 'gingerbread classical' style of many buildings in the southern United States. It is a proud frontage that proclaims the building's importance, reminding passers-by that this was Stoke's largest church, the heart of a successful Nonconformist movement.

At the back, the chapel is much more restrained but has a different, austere beauty. Its walls, which curve at the rear to form a broad, semicircular apse, are built entirely of brick in a striking chequerboard pattern. This is made in two different colours: red bricks, laid so that their long sides are showing, and yellow ones, laid so that their shorter ends, or headers, can be seen. As Ptolemy points out, this brickwork has suffered from years of pollution and is now blackened by soot and fumes. But in one place, where another structure was built against the walls and later demolished, the original bold effect can still be seen. The brilliant colours seem to sing out, and they would have looked sensational in the smoke-blackened atmosphere of industrial Stoke.

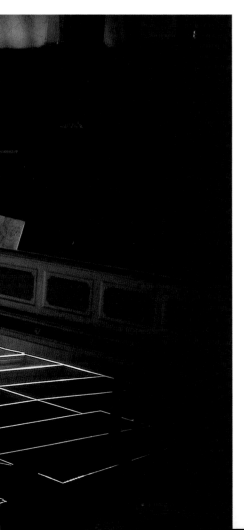

Inside is a surprisingly complete – and surprisingly rich – interior, with many fittings dating from the 1850s. The focus, as usual in dissenting chapels, is the pulpit. This is a huge construction, raised high, approached by very unusual twin curving stairs and topped by a large sounding board. It is clear that the sermon was the most important part of the services held here. Nearby is a complete mahogany communion rail and the communion pew, and above are the remains of a large and handsome organ.

The congregation sat in rows of pews, which also survive on the ground floor and above, in the curving gallery. For the most part everyone in the pews could see the pulpit. Although the gallery is supported by iron columns, the building's roof is a single span from wall to wall, without the need for extra pillars. This means that the view from the gallery itself is exceptionally good.

There is panelling everywhere, much of it in dark wood, but the interior is not dark because large windows, edged with stained glass but mostly clear, flood light into the building. Marianne notes how an ingenious curved profile to the undersides of the gallery frees up enough interior wall space to have large windows downstairs as well as up, so the spaces below the galleries – which were dark and dingy in many chapels – are here light and bright.

Bethesda Chapel was a thriving centre of worship throughout the Victorian period, although when Ridgway died in 1860 the New Connexion ended its period of fast expansion. A successful Sunday School brought young blood into the church and ensured that many children got the basics of an education at a time before schooling was available to all. Every Sunday, up to 3,000 worshippers packed the pews.

The twentieth century saw a decline in attendance, although there was a revival under a particularly charismatic minister during the 1950s. But in the following decades, with many potteries closing and church attendance generally falling, congregations got smaller. Bethesda finally closed at the end of 1985.

Since then the building has been empty and has become the victim of damp, structural movement and invading pigeons. Other problems, such as the 1970s ceiling of acoustic tiles, also need to be sorted out. But the chapel is still a storehouse of memories, evoked by items like the organist's file of music by such luminaries of the early twentieth century as the popular composer Samuel Coleridge-Taylor. Plans are afoot to put right the structural problems and to find roles for the building that will serve the local community, perhaps converting the rooms at the front of the chapel to office space for letting and using the church itself for concerts and occasional services. Local supporters look forward to the time when the great organ will resound again.

THE EAST

RESTORATION

'Coalhouse brings together the head and the heart of military history. The head is there in the engineering, and the heart because this was a fort manned by people. It sums up so much about the defence of this realm.'

Richard Holmes champions
COALHOUSE FORT

'Greyfriars Tower has obviously been a focus for people for generations. It is a curious and eccentric piece. The fact is it leans, and frankly we haven't got enough buildings that lean.'

John Peel champions
GREYFRIARS TOWER

'Moulton Mill provided employment and prosperity for this Lincolnshire town. It must be restored so that people will be able to see an eighteenth-century agricultural building in operation and understand something about the cycle of life at that time.'

Tim Wonnacott champions
MOULTON WINDMILL

'Very flat, Norfolk.' Noël Coward's blunt dismissal is often taken to stand for the whole of eastern England, from Lincolnshire to Essex. But it is only part of the story. There are low, rolling hills across much of East Anglia. In Suffolk and Essex, these hills are crossed by river valleys made famous by the paintings of Constable. Even Lincolnshire, also famed for flatness, has its Wolds, a range of chalky hills to the north of the county, which have their own beauty, little known to outsiders. Only in the watery regions of the fens and broads, stretching across parts of Norfolk, Cambridgeshire and southern Lincolnshire, is the country truly flat – an alluvial landscape of drains and dykes, with long horizons interrupted by the occasional windmill or church tower pointing defiantly at the broad, windswept sky.

The other generalization about the East is that it is isolated from the rest of Britain. Much of the area is well away from the main north–south routes, and the East has few major cities. Most travellers, to be sure, have little reason to come here. For much of its history, the north of the region was cut off from the rest of the country. For centuries the flatlands of the fens were only partially drained and presented to incomers a treacherous landscape of marshes and bogs dotted with islands where small towns and villages grew up. The major towns, such as Peterborough and Cambridge, were on the edge of the marshland. From the seventeenth century onwards, more drains were dug and the flat, fertile landscape of today evolved.

It is a different story in Essex, which is close to London and home to many who work in the capital. Essex also boasts a major port at Harwich and Stansted's international airport. Stansted's modern passenger terminal, designed by Sir Norman Foster, is popular with architects and travellers alike. And in times of war, from the Roman period to the twentieth century, Essex was far from isolated, playing a vital part in the defence of the capital against foreign invaders.

For most people, English history begins with the Romans and their invasion of the country in the first century AD. A key act of this invasion was the taking of Camulodunum, a major British centre that was to become Colchester. Buildings from virtually every period are still visible in Colchester, from Roman remains and a Norman castle to medieval churches and Georgian houses. This continuity suggests that, for all its isolation, eastern England has held its own through history, and this is reflected in remarkable buildings all over the region.

There is little good building stone in eastern England. There are exceptions, such as the part of south-western Lincolnshire where there is fine limestone, seen to perfection in the town of Stamford, with its streets and squares of the houses of Stuart and Georgian merchants beautifully detailed in local stone. But on the whole the builders of the East have had either to make do with stone that is difficult to work or to use other materials. For hundreds of years they have been turning this drawback on its head and producing buildings like no others.

The fens and flatlands are rich in clay, and so the main building material for houses, farms and 'working' buildings is brick. Many isolated farms and hamlets dot the landscape, and towns such as Spalding, set in the bulb-growing country of southern Lincolnshire, have rows of Georgian brick houses, both large and small. In the eastern part of the region, local clays produce attractive reddish-brown bricks. Further west lie the gault clays of Cambridgeshire and western Norfolk, which give yellow bricks. The abundant clay is also used to produce roofing tiles. For the most part these are pantiles, the curved tiles that give the roofs of houses in these parts their characteristic texture of ridges, as if they were covered with rows of terracotta pots. The warm shades of red or yellow bricks and rich red pantiles create a welcoming appearance in this often cold and windy area of the country.

Some of this brick architecture reflects a long-standing link between this area and the Netherlands. Dutch engineers, such as Cornelius Vermuyden, who was brought in by the Duke of Bedford, were involved in draining the fens. King's Lynn, the port on the Wash, maintained strong links with Holland, and some of the houses hereabouts have stepped and curved gables, just like Dutch buildings.

Much of Norfolk and Suffolk are chalklands, but the chalk is overlaid by layers of clay and flint. In many places flint, collected and mined since prehistoric times, became the traditional building material, and it gives a special character to a number of East Anglian villages. Nodules of flint look like pebbles on the outside, and some builders laid them like this to produce walls with the texture of a cobbled street. Another technique was to split the flint nodules in two to reveal their dark inner colour. Stoneworkers frequently broke lumps of flint in this way, shaping them to produce a flat, dark-grey surface. Often this is the part of the stones that is visible in a flint wall.

A good local source of limestone and its proximity to the Great North Road to London made Stamford rich and successful from the Middle Ages to the eighteenth century. Its limestone houses and churches still make it one of the most beautiful of all English towns.

A medieval church was meant to represent the whole of God's kingdom, so looking up we might expect to see the heavenly host. This was the notion behind the wooden roof of St Wendreda's church, March, Cambridgeshire, where dozens of carved angels look down on the congregation.

Flints can be used in regular courses, but on modest buildings, such as small houses, they are usually laid uncoursed to give a random surface of irregular, shining stones. At the corners and around doors and windows, bricks are used to strengthen the structure. Red or yellow bricks at the corners and ruddy pantiles on the roof contrast well with the grey flint walls of many a Norfolk house. In some places these houses are roofed in thatch rather than tiles. In both Norfolk and Suffolk, the favourite thatching material is Norfolk reed, which is long-lasting and grows in abundance in Norfolk's broads and marshes.

Further south, timber was more plentiful, as there were thick oak forests in the valleys of Essex and Suffolk, and a rich variety of timber-framed buildings is found in the area. In some places the timber frameworks and wattle-and-daub infill are visible, creating a pattern of dark and light. Towns like Lavenham, south-east of Bury St Edmunds, have many streets of these houses, some dating from the late Middle Ages.

But many of the early builders in this part of East Anglia did not want the timber frame to show, so they developed a whole style of building based on colourwashes and intricately decorated plasterwork. A Suffolk village can be a glowing mixture of different-coloured plastered walls, with neighbouring houses plastered in yellow, buff, apricot or even pink. There are also white houses, though these are more common to the west, in Cambridgeshire. Plastering the outsides of these timber-framed buildings both kept out the rain and insulated the interior so that it was warmer in winter and cooler in summer. But the glory of these houses, especially in many towns and villages in Essex, lies in the sheer art of the plasterer, in a technique of raised decoration called pargeting. Flowers and leaves, dates and initials, and all sorts of abstract patterns in low relief interlace their way across the outside walls of these houses.

Larger houses and castles were more likely to be built of stone. The Normans defended this remote area with some of their finest castles. Norman tower keeps, great solid masses of masonry, survive in several places, such as Hedingham, near Halstead in Essex, and Castle Rising, looking out towards the Wash near King's Lynn. Stone seemed the obvious choice for such large, high-status structures where both strength and appearance were important. But even castles and large houses could be made of brick. Tatershall Castle, near the northern edge of the Lincolnshire fens, is a great tower keep of the 1440s built almost entirely in red brick, an astonishing sight. And there are brick country houses, too, such as Norfolk's Blickling Hall, an enchanting composition of turrets, chimneys and curvaceous Dutch gables, again built almost completely of brick.

Just as outstanding and typical of East Anglia are the churches that dot the landscape. Many are ancient – Norfolk has a clutch of churches with round, flint-built towers, some dating back to Saxon times. Even more outstanding are the later-medieval churches, often enormous buildings serving tiny parishes. Built in the perpendicular style of the fifteenth century, these churches have rows of large windows, a vast nave for the congregation and a tall, square tower visible for miles. Inside, the timber roofs of churches like the ones at March and Elm, both in the flat country south of the Wash, can take the breath away with their rows of protruding hammer beams and ranks of carved angels. These amazing churches were built with the profits of a cloth trade that hit highs of prosperity in the late fourteenth and fifteenth centuries. Churches like those at Lavenham and Long Melford, both near Sudbury in Suffolk, are among the glories of English architecture. Norfolk has similarly stunning churches, such as those at Cawston and Salle, north-west of Norwich.

Some of the East Anglian churches have flint walls built using an outstanding decorative technique, a patterned effect called flushwork. In flushwork, the flint is combined with other stones to make patterns. The result looks rather like a large-scale version of a cabinet-maker's inlay. In the most elaborate examples, like the church of St Miles in Coslany, Norwich, the bands of stone imitate the patterns of window tracery all over the walls.

The eastern cathedrals are just as dazzling. Lincoln, with its three towers and its Angel Choir covered with carvings of the heavenly host, Ely, with its unique octagonal lantern tower alive with light and branching vaulting ribs, and Norwich, with its rows of imposing Norman arches – all are world-class buildings that show the importance and wealth of this part of England in the Middle Ages. These ancient cathedral cities are the major settlements of the East. In general, the area's isolation has meant that they have not grown to a huge size, although both Lincoln and Norwich were major centres in the Middle Ages. All have managed to keep some of their historical buildings – Lincoln in particular has an impressive group of Georgian houses along the narrow, steep streets around the cathedral. It also preserves two impressive early-medieval town houses with round-headed windows dating from Norman times. These were the homes of Jewish businessmen, among the richest people of their times.

Another town with a long history and unique architecture is Cambridge. Its most famous building is the chapel of King's College, a dazzling confection of pinnacles, tracery and fan vaulting. But just as absorbing are the quadrangles of the older colleges, such as St John's, Trinity, Clare and Queens', punctuated by lawns and backed by the idyllic River Cam.

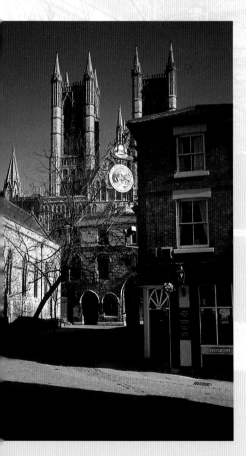

The gothic towers of Lincoln cathedral soar above the later buildings that crowd around them including the medieval Exchequer Gate, a sixteenth-century merchant's house and a Victorian pub front.

Clare College, Cambridge, has a west front dating from the late seventeenth century. Its tall square chimneys, parapet with balusters and giant classical columns are all typical of its period.

But many eastern towns and villages have a more utilitarian atmosphere than Cambridge. Towns such as Spalding were the centres for fertile farming country. They had markets where farmers from round about brought their corn and cattle. They also had windmills, where corn from the great fields of East Anglia was ground into flour. Mills have been part of the life of the East for centuries. In the valleys of Essex and Suffolk many water mills survive, cousins of the one at Flatford in Constable's most famous painting. In the flatlands, windmills were built to take advantage of the winds that blew uninterrupted across the broad, unsheltered fens.

The earliest type of windmill is the post mill. This type is made of wood, and the whole mill is rotated to turn the sails into the wind. Examples survive at Saxtead Green, near Framlingham in Suffolk, and at Bourn, a few miles west of Cambridge. But more common are the tower mills, which have their sails mounted on a wooden cap atop a round brick tower. On a tower mill only the sails and cap turn to face the wind. All over East Anglia the remains of these mills can be seen, gaunt brick towers beside canals and dykes. Viewed from after, these stark towers seem to be symbols of East Anglia's past, when wind power was vital to the area's economy. But some of the mills have been restored and bring in income in a different way – by attracting visitors, who can watch corn being ground just as it was in the eighteenth century. Meanwhile, wind power is being put to new uses, with the creation of several wind farms in the area. Their turning blades show once again that the East can make good use of its flat land and chilly breezes.

Coalhouse Fort EAST TILBURY

A modern Tower of London

ABOVE LEFT *Set in a wall of large granite blocks, the main entrance to Coalhouse Fort looks as strong as it did 130 years ago.*

ABOVE RIGHT *Among the historical treasure trove in the fort are First World War searchlights, their lenses still glinting as if ready to throw a dazzling beam across the estuary.*

OPPOSITE *The walkway running around the courtyard is supported on plain, circular columns, designed to be functional, but appearing very elegant.*

From the outside it looks indestructible. A great curving mass of granite, ragstone and concrete by the Thames in Essex, Coalhouse Fort has stood like a sentinel against foreign invasion since the 1870s. Built to defeat a possible French attack, it played a part in both the First and Second World Wars before the military left in 1946. It still contains many features and fittings from its main periods of operation.

In the mid-nineteenth century, war looked likely in Europe. The French were developing powerful, ironclad steamships and it seemed possible that they would invade England by sailing up the Thames and attacking London. In 1859 a Royal Commission recommended the construction of more than seventy forts and batteries across the country. Special stress was laid on improving the defences of the Thames estuary, and Coalhouse at East Tilbury was one of three new forts that were built to do so.

Building work proceeded slowly, with much stopping and starting, and the fort was not finally completed until the early 1870s. But what emerged was a new type of fortress – a vast bulwark containing a range of granite-faced, iron-shielded gun chambers called casemates, backed by barracks made of brick and Kentish ragstone at the rear. The walls of the gun battery were twenty feet thick – strong enough to resist the heaviest French bombardment – and concrete was used in the construction. Concrete had twin advantages: it was fireproof, and if it did break up in an attack it would crack into small fragments rather than falling in large, dangerous chunks.

The guns in the casemates were the biggest available at the time. Each weighed thirty-eight tons and fired half-ton projectiles towards the Thames. These rifled muzzle-loading guns were so powerful that their heavy shot could travel up to five miles. They were slow, heavy and noisy, but they would have made short work of an ironclad warship.

Approaching Coalhouse Fort by road, you see straight away that this is a strongly fortified building. Heavy iron-studded gates bar the way. Marianne notices especially the thick stone walls, dotted with small gun ports, splayed to allow a marksman to aim. But the real defences are on the river side, where the main attack was expected. Towards the river is a broad moat separated by a strip of land from an inner dry ditch. As well as the big guns, which were aimed at ships on the river, defenders could fire handguns, rifles or machine guns at an enemy trying to cross the ditch. These weapons were fired from the barrack windows, which were covered with inner bulletproof steel shutters pierced with firing holes. This system of multiple fortifications was vital because if the Thames forts fell, an invader could take London and would soon be in control of the whole country. Without such forts, as Ptolemy remarks, Britain could have become a province of France.

From the inside, the sheer mass of the fortifications becomes clear. Looking out of the loopholes you can see the thickness of the casemate walls, although the weight of the masonry above is concealed by elegant brick-vaulted ceilings. The vaults each have a hole through which smoke could escape, a reminder that conditions inside would have been appalling when the guns were being fired. Deafening noise, thick black smoke and guns recoiling eight or nine feet as they fired would have made life grim for the gunners. The men had to scream at the moment of firing, to relieve the pressure in their ears. Even so, most gunners were very deaf indeed. When an attack was threatened, the men slept by their guns so there was no relief from the Spartan conditions.

Inside the main courtyard, the barracks come as a surprise, for their inner walls are built not of granite but of bricks. These two-storey blocks contained accommodation for the garrison, storerooms, a hospital and even quarters where married soldiers and their wives could live during peacetime. Their yellow stock-brick walls and sash windows would have been just about the only thing that reminded the inhabitants of their homes in London.

The French invasion did not materialize, so the great guns were never fired at an enemy. But the British government kept Coalhouse Fort going as an insurance against future threats. By the time of the First World War it had more modern guns and a pair of large electrically powered searchlights to aid night firing. A minefield was also set up in the area. In 1940 there was once

Although the basic structure of the fort is solid, many details, such as the roofs above the walkway and some of the window frames, need replacement.

The great curving vaults of the casemates are visible from the yard. These large structures must have taken millions of bricks to build as the masonry is so thick.

Fire buckets stand ready, just as they did in times of war.

more a threat of invasion. This time the fort was equipped with anti-aircraft guns. It also became the control centre of the river minefield, and a special concrete pillbox was built for this purpose. After the war, Coalhouse saw brief service as a naval training centre and later as a store for a footwear manufacturer before conservation work began in the 1980s.

There is plenty of evidence of the fort's later use. The high-powered searchlights that illuminated the river at night during the First World War are preserved. With their metal shields, they burned brightly all night long to detect attacking vessels on the river. Their bombproof emplacements on the fort's roof command a long, broad vista over Essex and the Thames. These concrete emplacements look like the stark, white architecture of the 1930s, an example of military technology anticipating what happened later in the civilian world.

The Second World War has also left its mark on the site. Anti-aircraft guns remain, a reminder that by 1940 the main threat was from the air. And there is also the pillbox that acted as nerve centre for the mining operation on the river. Its stark concrete construction is high-quality work. Foursquare and pierced by slits and splayed openings, its design reminds Ptolemy of the brutalist concrete buildings of the 1960s, another odd glance towards the future.

The fort's project management committee are seeking funding for restoration and to make the fort an attractive and informative place to visit. There are plans to restore the barracks area as a visitor centre, with education facilities and a range of services for visitors. Anyone coming to the complex would learn much about the building's unique fortifications and its strategic position at the 'gateway' to London. Its special role in the warfare of the nineteenth and twentieth centuries makes Coalhouse Fort a modern Tower of London.

Moulton Windmill MOULTON

A towering monument to the miller's trade

Items like this sack remind visitors of the Biggadike family, who ran the mill for three generations.

You can't miss Moulton Windmill. At ninety-eight feet tall, it towers over everything around it. Even without its sails, it is the pride of Moulton, the village where it ground corn for some 170 years. Its brickwork still retains its beauty and its walls are full of milling memorabilia, from the stones and milling machinery to the bills in the office desk drawers. Many would like to restore the mill and see it grind corn once again. With its sails replaced, it would be the tallest windmill in Britain.

During the nineteenth century there were about ten thousand working windmills in Britain; now there are only fifty-three. Many were in eastern England, where the flat countryside and strong easterly winds made wind power a practical proposition. This was a rural area where most people relied on the land for their livelihood – they were farmers, farm workers or worked in allied businesses. Since many farmers grew corn, milling was one of the most important of these trades. A good miller was an asset to the community, and his mill was often in the middle of the village.

The mill at Moulton was built in 1820. By making it so tall, its builder, Robert King, ensured that its sails would catch the wind sooner and turn for longer. This type of mill is called a tower mill. It consists of a round brick tower topped with a wooden-framed cap, the part that holds the sails. The cap could turn so that the sails could be moved to face into the wind. The cap also held a second, much smaller, sail called a fantail. When the wind direction changed, the fantail caught the wind and pushed the cap around, so that the mill could carry on working.

For much of the Victorian period, the mill's sails turned as they were designed to do. But in 1895 disaster struck. One night, after a period of calm, a sudden wind blew up – from exactly the opposite direction from the wind that had last blown the sails around. Because the wind came suddenly, from the wrong direction, the mill's fantail could not turn the sails and the gale buffeted the backs of the sails. The noise of the gale woke the miller, who ran to the mill to try to turn the sails by hand. But he was too late – the wind was already blowing the sails off, and soon they lay in pieces on the ground.

And so Moulton Mill began a new phase in its history. A steam engine was installed to turn the stones and soon the mill was working again. Further upgrades to diesel and finally electricity were made, and three generations of

ABOVE LEFT *From paperwork and a typewriter of the early twentieth century to a 1990s 'No smoking' sign, the building contains relics of more than a century of milling and dealing in corn and flour.*

ABOVE CENTRE *Trapdoors open so that the hoist can lift sacks of grain to an upper floor of the mill, ready to be ground into flour.*

ABOVE RIGHT *One set of mill stones, connected to their shaft, wait as if ready to start working again while a spare stone leaning against a wall displays its beautifully dressed surface.*

the Biggadike family worked as millers for most of the twentieth century. In 1995 the last of the three, John Biggadike, retired, and because he had no heir to take over the business the mill finally closed.

From the outside, the mill is impressive. As well as being tall, the tower is beautifully built. For most of its height it is made of well-laid yellow bricks, but at the very top and bottom are red bricks, to give the tower a visual 'top and tail', described by Ptolemy as mirroring the proportions of classical architecture. The neat brickwork is especially impressive because the bricks were laid without scaffolding. The builders worked from the inside, installing the floors as they went up. It must have taken special care to lay the bricks from the inside out, finishing off each bed of mortar with perfect neatness.

Inside, things are just as impressive. The wooden beams are finished with precisely cut grooves and the banister rail is turned on a lathe. All the details have the stamp of quality. But more impressive even than this is the treasure-trove of machinery and equipment that is preserved inside the mill. Most of the mechanism that linked the sails to the millstones is still there, reminding the visitor that this whole huge structure existed mainly to link the sails to the great millstones, enabling them to turn and grind the corn.

Eight floors up, at the top of the mill, is the main wheel, called the 'wallower'. This is a vast horizontal wheel with large wooden cogs that originally engaged with another large cogwheel on the shaft that held the sails. From the wallower, the mill's huge central drive shaft passes vertically down through the floors to level four. Here, at the lower end of the shaft, another big cogwheel engages with two smaller wheels linked to the stones

The force of gravity takes flour away from the millstones down a wooden chute towards a waiting sack.

themselves. Two stones are in position, as if ready to grind another batch of grain. Other millstones stand nearby, their perfectly finished surfaces showing how carefully a millstone had to be made. The stones must be well balanced and cut with grooves to allow the flour to make its way to the edge of the stones and out through the narrow gap between them.

The power from the turning sails was harnessed in other ways. A sack hoist, still here with its original chain drive, was connected to the shaft, so that heavy sacks of grain could be lifted up the tower with a minimum of effort. Much other original machinery remains, as do some of the later additions: for example, the electric milling machine used by miller John Biggadike during the mill's last working years. A well-appointed office survives, together with much surviving paperwork from different periods in the mill's history – gold dust for the industrial historian.

The superb workmanship of Moulton Windmill shows that it was built by a man who meant his work to last. Robert King, the original builder, was convinced that his mill would be at the centre of village life for centuries. As Marianne comments, nineteenth-century builders took pride in their creations and expected them to last. It is hoped to restore the building fully, replace the sails, open it to visitors as a working museum and bring it back to the heart of village life. When its millstones turn again and organic flour is ground here, England's tallest windmill will be a source of pride for locals and a source of education and nourishment for those who come to see it.

Greyfriars Tower KING'S LYNN

The leaning tower of Lynn

ABOVE LEFT *A tall stone arch with simple carved mouldings led into the crossing or walking space beneath Greyfriars Tower.*

ABOVE RIGHT *Tracery, the intricate patterned stonework that divides the windows, is the main form of ornament on the tower itself.*

OPPOSITE *The surprisingly slender lines of the tower and its hexagonal shape are two features that make the structure unusual.*

The towers of King's Lynn stand out proud in the flat Norfolk landscape, looking out to the sea. The twin towers of St Margaret's Church and the single one of St Nicholas's are imposing, but most striking of all is Greyfriars Tower, fragile, isolated and set at a slight angle that makes it, for some, the 'leaning tower of Lynn'.

Greyfriars Tower was part of King's Lynn's medieval Franciscan friary. It is one of only three surviving friary towers in the country and the best of the trio, with its delicate Gothic windows, intriguing carvings, narrow stair turret and unusual hexagonal shape. The tower is in a poor state of repair and is out of bounds to visitors – it badly needs restoring.

The Franciscan order, known as the Greyfriars because of the colour of the robes they wore, were founded by St Francis of Assisi in the thirteenth century. Like all monks, they took vows of poverty, chastity and obedience, but for the friars poverty had a special meaning – they relied totally on alms for their food and upkeep. The special work of the friars was preaching, and they travelled widely, often attracting many listeners because of their entertaining oratory. They were also notable scholars, so it is not surprising that after they arrived in England they were especially active in the university towns of Oxford and Cambridge.

The friars probably arrived in King's Lynn in the 1230s and soon established themselves as part of the influential group of Franciscan preachers and

The masonry of the gable beneath the tower is in two distinct parts. The lower section is made up of small, neat stones that would have been visible inside the church. The upper section, however, is of rough, rather crude-looking stonework as it would have been hidden between the ceiling and the outer covering of the roof.

scholars in the Cambridge area. They would have built a friary soon after arriving, but extended and improved the building several times over the centuries. Apart from the tower, very little of the friary remains, but, as Marianne points out, it would originally have been at the centre of a large complex. The tower was part of the church, and this was next to a cloister that was surrounded by the buildings where the friars lived: a refectory for eating, a dormitory for sleeping, storerooms, a guesthouse, rooms where they could study, and so on.

The tower was added in the fifteenth century over the passage, or 'walking place', between the nave and chancel of the friary church. Like other friary towers, it is slender and may have contained only a single bell to call people to services. More than anything else, the friars probably built it to emulate the other church towers that had sprung up around their friary, to show that they, too, could raise a tall building to God's glory.

The community of friars seems to have thrived until the 1530s, when Henry VIII closed England's monasteries down. In 1538 the friars were driven out and the church and other buildings were razed to the ground. Much of the stone was probably carted away and reused in other buildings. Only the tower was allowed to stay and, as the town's tallest building, acted as a welcome seamark for shipping out at sea.

The tower is built in a mixture of stone and brick. It now looks rather a hotchpotch, although the overall shape of the tower and its windows are elegantly designed in the perpendicular Gothic style. But originally, when the tower was surrounded by other parts of the friary and church, it would have looked more ordered, and most of the brick would have been concealed by other bits of the structure. Drawing the tower, Ptolemy notices another feature that makes it look slightly odd: the main arch is positioned off-centre. This is due to the way the church was altered over the centuries and, again, would not have been obvious when the building was complete. The tower must have started to lean as it was being built. A close look at its outline shows that the upper portion is closer to the vertical than the rest of the tower, so the builders must have corrected the lean as they worked.

In the space under the tower its fine vault can be seen, made of brick but with strong stone ribs holding it together like a skeleton. Climbing up to look closely at the vault, one can see details that would probably have been invisible to the friars standing on the floor below. Most astonishing are the carvings – some of them truly grotesque – on the corbels, the stones that support the ribs of the vault. A long-eared bat, a long-toothed devil, a woman in an elaborate headdress and a man apparently sitting on a privy are all featured in these carvings. It is hard to know why the masons chose these subjects. Was it to remind the friars of their vows, the woman recalling their vow of chastity and the bat symbolizing the devil? Or was it simply to play a sly trick on the friars, who could not see the carvings anyway? The answer was lost with the carvers.

One thing is plain, though: traces of ancient colouring reveal that these sculptures were originally painted. The fragments of paint are a reminder that medieval churches were usually covered with wall paintings. After the Reformation in the sixteenth century, Protestants plastered over nearly all of these murals, and in many churches Victorian restorers scraped off the plaster and removed the hidden paintings for good at the same time.

Greyfriars Tower was built over 500 years ago and has been a ruin for more than 400 years. As Marianne says, it is an 'all-or-nothing' building: it has to be restored before it becomes dangerous and collapses completely. So the aim is to stabilize the structure, at the same time carrying out an archaeological investigation of the site and providing information for visitors. The tower's venerable age, its unusual history and its beauty make it a worthy ancient monument. But it is more than this. It speaks to us eloquently of an age when communities were sure enough of their faith to dedicate their tallest, most glorious buildings to God.

Shorn of its surrounding structures, the tower is now supported by massive stone buttresses that help to prevent the building from leaning any more than it does already.

'Bank Hall is an extraordinary building that encapsulates the whole history of stately homes. It can tell us not just about the grand folk who lived there, but about the whole texture of life in the country.'

Loyd Grossman champions
BANK HALL

'The communal nature of the Victoria Baths is what makes it unique as a historical building. It is something that everybody could use on a daily basis and wouldn't be like any other baths in the rest of Britain.'

Richard E. Grant champions
VICTORIA BATHS

'Brackenhill Tower is in the Border territory, which in the 1500s was as near to the Wild West as Britain ever got. There are no written records, so if we lose it, we lose a part of our history.'

Martin Bell champions
BRACKENHILL TOWER

n the nineteenth century the spectacular mountain scenery of the Lake District became fashionable for the first time. Writers such as the Romantic poets William Wordsworth and Samuel Taylor Coleridge celebrated the dramatic contours of mountains and the blue waters of lakes because such landscape seemed to express better than anything the sublime grandeur of nature. As a result of these writers' enthusiasm, the far north-west of the country, with its mountains, crags, tarns and passes, became the byword for beautiful scenery on a grand scale.

To the east of the Lake District, the great mountain chain of the Pennines offers views that are just as striking. But here the mountains are punctuated by the Yorkshire Dales, a farming area of steep-sided valleys and charming villages where the landscape is on a more intimate and hospitable scale than either the Pennines or Cumbria. To the south, Cumbria gives way to Lancashire, a county known as one of the cradles of industry but which nevertheless has its rural areas too – notably the moorland of the Forest of Bowland. The scenery of the North West is as varied as any in England.

The North West is on the fringes of England, far from London's gravitational pull. Yet it has been a place of action and conflict at least since the time of the Romans. The great wall built by Hadrian's army starts at Carlisle, and it is still a famous symbol of the tensions between England and Scotland. Romans and Picts, the armies of medieval England and Scotland, and raiders like the reivers, notorious robbers and kidnappers of the late Middle Ages, fought among the windy uplands of the north-western borders. Castles in major towns, such as Carlisle and Penrith, together with many smaller fortified houses, remain to tell the story of these turbulent times. But the region also has its share of more peaceful buildings, traditional farms and cottages that show how builders used the materials that were available nearby.

In Cumbria the landscape is so spectacular that it is easy to miss the architecture. The buildings here are modest for the most part, typically long, low houses, often whitewashed and sometimes joined to plain stone barns. Where the stone has been left bare, Lakeland's cottages and farmhouses can glow in the sun, displaying a range of colours from grey and blue to purple and brown. Green slate, pinkish-grey granite and red sandstone create this varied display of colours, and in some places the colour scheme is livened up even more with paint and render, the walls white or pastel-coloured, the door

ABOVE LEFT *High above Ambleside in Cumbria is the Kirkstone Pass Inn. Its low white-rendered stone walls, small, inset windows, and slate roof combine to offer protection from the cold winds.*

ABOVE RIGHT *The thick Norman walls of Carlisle Castle look forbidding, but parts of the interior at least are more welcoming – a number of the rooms have been fitted out as they would have been in the time of the castle's medieval constable.*

and window surrounds picked out in brighter shades. Paint, render and stone are often neighbours, giving a polychrome variety to villages such as Dufton and Milburn on the Cumbrian edge of the Pennines.

The walls of these Cumbrian houses can have a rich and unusual texture. While huge rocks are often used above windows and doors, and to reinforce the corners of a building, small, thin pieces of green slate may be used for the rest of the wall. The mortar between these stones is not spread flush with the wall surface, but is kept well back so that a narrow furrow runs between each piece of stone. This creates a pattern of light and shadow that gives the walls their special grain.

From their bleak high uplands to the nearby lush lowlands, the Pennines present another landscape of contrasts. But beneath this variety lies a rock used widely in building hereabouts: the tough, coarse stone known as millstone grit, or gritstone. This material, actually a form of sandstone, ranges widely in colour, but pollution blackens it and so it is often thought of as a dark rock. Its sombre tones play a leading part in forming the character of this part of the North West.

Millstone grit comes out of the quarry in outsize pieces, so houses are often built of big blocks. It is common to see windows surrounded by just four long stones, two uprights and two horizontals, a feature that gives local buildings a weighty quality. Field walls are similarly massive, standing out dark grey against the green grass of this sheep country. For hundreds of years, people here made their livings in the wool trade, either as sheep farmers or as weavers working from home. Cloth weavers needed light, so old houses in these parts often have long strips of windows to let in the sun.

A wall of big chunks of dark-grey rock could be forbidding, especially when roofed in the traditional way with the same dark material in the form of

Narrow, lancet-shaped windows line the clock tower of Manchester Town Hall, a Victorian homage to the medieval early gothic style.

gritstone flags. But it need not be so. Many builders use lighter mortar between the dark stones, which gives their walls contrast, pattern and a quality akin to op art. Small Lancashire houses can also dazzle with brilliant paintwork. On one house, bright white window surrounds might stand out against a background of an almost black gritstone wall; on another, the masonry around the window is painted black while the window frames themselves are picked out in white; in yet another, yellow details contrast with darker walls. Effects like these brighten even a drab northern winter.

To the east, in the Dales, the landscape is softer and the buildings seem to match. The prevailing material is a pale-grey limestone that is used both for houses and for field walls. The houses themselves are often low and long and next to farm buildings. The pale colour, seen everywhere from the walls of houses to the outcrops that supplied the building material, gives the area a lighter palette than in the dark, millstone grit country. The clusters of farm buildings, often with houses and barns linked, are at one with the landscape. With their long, low lines and brown-stone roofs, they have many charming features, not least the door lintel carved with the date and the initials of the owner and his wife.

When it comes to larger houses, the architecture of the North West is just as varied. One pattern is the fashion for large, ornate, timber-framed houses. Similar to the black and white houses of the neighbouring north Midlands, they are just as flamboyant. Rufford Old Hall near Ormskirk is a prominent example. Its outer walls are covered in the black and white patterns of timbers, repeated inside in the magnificent great hall, which has changed little since Tudor times.

Many of the larger houses are stone-built, and they come in a variety of styles, from Elizabethan mansions such as Levens Hall, south of Kendal, to late Victorian country houses. A number of these developed from castles as the unrest that plagued the area started to die down at the end of the Middle Ages. Levens Hall itself is a house with pale stone walls and mullioned windows, but it is built around the remains of a fortified tower of the thirteenth century. Muncaster Castle, near the Cumbrian coast, has a similar story – a medieval tower that grew into a country house with the addition of wings as the desire for privacy and luxury became more important than the need for defence.

These great country houses owed their existence mainly to agricultural wealth. But a new source of income began to emerge as the North West saw the beginnings of Britain's Industrial Revolution. The canals and railways that made industry possible, bringing fuel to the factories and taking away manufactured goods, came here early. By 1761, James Brindley's

Bridgewater Canal was bringing cheap coal from the Duke of Bridgewater's mine at Worsley to Manchester, a market town that was turning into a centre of the cotton industry. Liverpool was becoming a thriving port, receiving raw materials and exporting finished goods. The two cities were connected by the Liverpool and Manchester Railway, which opened in 1830 and was the first to use only steam power to haul its trains. The two cities in their different ways have become symbols of the 'Industrial North', and their remarkable nineteenth-century buildings reflect the fact.

The rise of Manchester is mirrored in its town hall, a masterpiece of Victorian Gothic designed by Alfred Waterhouse and built between 1867 and 1876. With its enormous clock tower and its façade of pointed arches, it is an image of the city's importance. This is confirmed by the decorative details, all of which point to the industry that brought success to Manchester – there are mosaics both of cotton plants and industrious bees, and murals by Ford Madox Brown telling the story of the city. Railway stations and great public buildings such as the City Art Gallery and the Free Trade Hall are among the other lasting legacies of Manchester's nineteenth-century expansion.

To the west, Liverpool has another stunning collection of Victorian civic buildings, such as St George's Hall (originally combining a concert hall with law courts), the Walker Art Gallery and the County Museum. But in their way, even more impressive are the warehouses of Liverpool's Albert Dock. These great foursquare, red-brick structures, built in the 1840s, were the centre of Liverpool's trade during the second half of the nineteenth century. They were innovative buildings, with roofs made of iron plates, floors separated by brick vaults supported on wrought-iron beams, and brick walls reinforced at the corners with granite. Tough, fireproof and with a functional elegance all their own, they have survived to live a new life as offices, museums, restaurants and television studios.

These great cities were centres of trade, where shiploads of goods came and went every day. At Halifax, a textile town since the Middle Ages, one can still see the place where cloth was traded. This is the magnificent eighteenth-century Piece Hall, so called because it was the place where pieces of cloth were bought and sold. The building is based on an Italianate stone courtyard with rows of classical columns. Behind this elegant frontage are 315 merchants' rooms, where the buying and selling took place. This enormous courtyard is the only surviving cloth market of this period and is a reminder of the power and wealth of the northern wool merchants.

Liverpool's Albert Dock combines tough, functional brick and granite with tapering classical columns.

At Port Sunlight one way in which the designers made the environment more pleasant than the norm in late nineteenth-century industrial towns was by creating stepped-back façades that left room for greenery in front of the houses.

There is also plenty of evidence in the North West of the manufacturing industries that fuelled this trade. The remains of mills, mines, pumping stations and engine houses dot the landscape of Lancashire. It is difficult to imagine now that these places would have been alive with the noise and movement of the different processes of the textile industry – the production of cotton yarn with machines such as spinning jennies and spinning mules, the weaving of cloth with flying shuttles, and fabric finishing with great water- and steam-powered hammers. The buildings that housed these machines, for the most part simple brick structures with rows of windows, were the pumping hearts of the Victorians' great empire, the engines that made possible the wealth and civic pride of Liverpool and Manchester. Many of these buildings have been demolished, and a number have been converted to modern uses. But one weaving mill, Burnley's Queen Street Mill, survives to show visitors what these factories were like when they were working. It houses several hundred looms, still powered by a great compound steam engine of 1895.

Life for the workers in most of these mills was grim. Most returned to poor conditions in cramped houses, and personal hygiene was a tin bath in the kitchen – or a weekly trip to the public baths. The middle classes, though, had better housing in leafy suburbs that were built in the late nineteenth century around the major cities. One visionary industrialist, soap manufacturer William Hesketh Lever, wanted better for his workers. He built the village of Port Sunlight on the Wirral peninsula to provide a higher standard of living for his employees. The first plans were drawn up in 1888. They revealed spacious, cottage-style houses in landscaped surroundings, and the quality of the building won over the workers as they began to move in. Port Sunlight also impressed later town planners, influencing the garden suburb movement that transformed many city fringes in the early twentieth century. Once again, in planning as in industry, the North West was at the cutting edge.

Bank Hall CHORLEY

A home of Lancashire lords

ABOVE LEFT *In the early twentieth century, Bank Hall presented a romantic façade of tall chimneys, ornate gables and the clock tower of 1608.*

ABOVE RIGHT *The hall's main doors, with their original ironwork, now stand inside the house, waiting to be refitted.*

OPPOSITE *The hall's builders picked out details such as window surrounds, corners and parapets in sandstone.*

The Jacobean period of the early seventeenth century produced one of the liveliest styles of British architecture. Walls of hand-made bricks glow in the sunshine in a range of reds and browns. Skylines are alive with stone knobs and finials. Gables, curved and stepped, make dramatic silhouettes. Bank Hall, at Brotherton near Chorley in Lancashire, home successively of the Banastre and Legh Keck families, is a radiant example of the style.

The present house was begun in 1608, by either William Banastre of Banke or his son, Henry, who later became Member of Parliament for Preston. His builders used traditional, local materials – mainly bricks made nearby. As Ptolemy notes, these were available in different colours, and the builders made diamond patterns with them to decorate the walls. They also used sandstone for the details and Cumberland slate for the roofs. These materials were common enough on all sorts of buildings hereabouts. But the style of Bank Hall was the latest fashion, all curvaceous gables and stone finials, the sort of thing that was already familiar in southern England but brand new in the north. The elegant gables have a Dutch feel, testimony to contacts between England and the Netherlands. Such details look attractive in the low, flat landscapes of Holland and East Anglia, where they stand out against the sky. Here in Lancashire, too, the land is low-lying, and the house makes a memorable landmark.

Inside, the house would have been just as striking, with the main rooms panelled in oak and topped with ornate plaster ceilings. It looked, and was,

Not all recent visitors have been welcome. Trespassers have been damaging the house for thirty years.

Although many of the walls are sound, most of the roof covering has long since disappeared.

sumptuous – only a couple of generations earlier, this kind of interior decoration was the preserve of the richest grandees.

Like many English country house owners, the Banastre family were keen builders who improved and extended their home. In 1660 Christopher Banastre was appointed High Sheriff of Lancashire, and it was probably at around this time that he added two features to the houses that reflect his status, two real architectural 'statements'. The first was the tower, which provides beautiful views over the surrounding countryside and also marks out Bank Hall as the important house of an important person. Its slightly thicker brickwork shows that it was built at a different date from the rest of the house.

Inside, miraculously surviving among the dereliction, is Christopher's second addition: the grand staircase. The superb craftsmanship of its fat, turned balusters and heavy carved-oak handrail impresses Ptolemy. But the supporting structure is even more amazing – the stair treads are held only at one end, where they are fixed into the surrounding walls; the other ends hang free, suspended in mid-air. We are used to seeing such cantilevered structures in modern buildings, but in the seventeenth century a cantilevered staircase was something new, and must have amazed and impressed the hall's many visitors.

Bank Hall's second heyday began in the early nineteenth century. Farmers were doing well, and local estates benefited from the high prices brought about by the Napoleonic Wars. The owner of Bank Hall, George Anthony Legh Keck, was soon looking to upgrade the hall to the new lavish standards of the time. By now, the house was looked after by an army of domestic servants, from the butler and housekeeper to a number of grooms and maids. Bank Hall needed better servants' quarters and bigger rooms in which to entertain the family's guests. In 1832 it got both – a huge service wing to the east and enlarged reception rooms to the west. The house almost doubled in size.

The architect for the extension, George Webster of Kendal, chose bricks to harmonize with the existing fabric. But the nineteenth-century bricks are easy to tell from the earlier ones. While the Jacobean bricks are rough-surfaced and display a variety of sizes and colours, the later bricks are smooth, uniform in colour and regular in size. You do not need the dated lead hoppers at the tops of the drainpipes to tell which parts of the house were built in 1832.

Heaps of architectural fragments, the result of attacks from the weather, encroaching ivy and trespassers, now litter the ground floor of Bank Hall. Chimneystacks, bits of fallen floor and ceiling, plasterwork, bricks, stone and timbers are everywhere in pieces. Even the hall's original Jacobean oak main door, studded with iron reinforcing nails, is propped up against a wall inside.

But among the debris, a lot survives to bring the rooms to life. In the huge Victorian kitchen, ranges and work areas still peep between the rubble, and one can imagine the vast spaces full of hurrying cooks and maids. At the other end of the house, the three-floor nineteenth-century extension is open to the sky, but the walls of each storey can be seen at a glance, revealing how the house worked in layers: servants' rooms at the top in the low-ceilinged attic, grand bedrooms with plaster decoration for the guests below, and an even grander ballroom for lavish parties on the ground floor.

The parties continued well into the twentieth century, and there were famous gatherings during Grand National week, when British royalty visited

ABOVE LEFT *Rubble, timbers and lengths of old wiring wait to fall.*

ABOVE RIGHT *Many surviving fragments, such as this section of a clock face and piece of moulding offer vital clues about decorative features that have been destroyed.*

and the Aga Khan stayed. The hall was also, like many country houses, a centre for local people, employing many of them, and putting on family social events. After all, it was the community that ran and maintained houses like Bank Hall, and even built them in the first place. Owners did their best, in a paternalistic way, for the scores of retainers and their families.

Like many other large houses, the hall was used by troops during the Second World War. After the war, there was neither the money nor the appetite for the lavish lifestyle of earlier years, and many country houses were simply demolished. Bank Hall has survived – just. But it has lost its roof and, as the rain, frost and vegetation attack it, Marianne senses that it cannot last long in this state. The Bank Hall Action Group is working for the hall's restoration. One day, it hopes to open part of the restored building to visitors and to make the rest available to the charity Autism Initiatives, which wants to open a training centre for young autistic adults on the site.

Brackenhill Tower LONGTOWN

A refuge of border raiders

Worn but proud, the family coat of arms is still set high on one outside wall of the Tower.

OPPOSITE *A detail of the tower's exterior shows the solid construction. Big, smoothly dressed stones were used at the corners, more roughly hewn blocks for the rest of the walls. Most of this stone is still in good condition, although damp, time and lack of maintenance have taken their toll on the mortar joints.*

It was border country, and life was dangerous. The English and Scottish had been fighting it out for hundreds of years. By the sixteenth century the two countries were supposed to be at peace, but there was still unrest. In this difficult atmosphere, families had to tough it out and survive as best they could. For many, this meant reiving – in other words, stealing. Cattle rustling, kidnapping, blackmail, protection rackets – they were all endemic here as one clan preyed on another before hotfooting it back home and barring the door against attackers. So for a reiver family, home had to be safer than houses.

One of the most notorious of these families were the Grahams, whose base was Brackenhill Tower. Today, the tower is in England, near the Cumbrian border. In the sixteenth century it was in a feared no man's land called the Debatable Land. Anyone who travelled in the Debatable Land risked robbery and worse. So at Brackenhill the Grahams built themselves a formidable fortress.

At the base of the tower, the walls are about five feet thick and built of solid stone. Ptolemy suggests that some of the blocks may be so large they span the entire thickness of the wall, holding it together like the header courses in brickwork. It is awesomely massive masonry. Today, the tower looks especially tough and rough because the stones were chiselled into an irregular surface. As Marianne explains, this was to act as a key for harling, the traditional Scottish render of lime mortar and pebbles with which nearly the whole of the tower, apart from cornerstones and window surrounds, was covered. Only a few tiny traces of harling remain.

The tower is topped by a crenellated parapet, just like a medieval castle. A lookout would have patrolled there, peering through one of the gaps in the parapet, known as crenels and dodging behind one of the uprights if he saw anyone coming. If any enemy approached, the lookout would sound the alarm and soon several armed men would be waiting, ready to shoot.

If anyone got near enough to the tower to try to force his way in, he would have had his work cut out. The doors were made of thick, solid oak, reinforced with iron studs, hung on heavy hinges and secured with massive locks. If any attackers somehow got past these barriers, they found themselves in a cramped space at the base of a narrow stone staircase. Only one attacker at a time could enter this small area, and the occupants could easily pick each one off.

It was also hard to force an entry into the tower's vaulted basement. This was the storeroom where stolen goods and cattle could be hidden safely and out of the way of any owner who rashly came to try to claim his possessions back.

Another of the Grahams' houses even had an underground passage connecting such a basement store with the family's pastures. At Brackenhill, the stolen goods had to come in through the door but, once in, they were secure.

ABOVE LEFT *The tower is not a tall structure – just high enough to provide a secure refuge and a decent look-out post.*

ABOVE RIGHT *There is little in the way of decoration in this utilitarian building, but the Grahams did allow themselves some restrained carved moulding on the stone door surround.*

Ritchie Graham, who built the main tower at Brackenhill after he inherited the property in 1584, was one of the most feared of the reivers. But there were many others. The Grahams held thirteen towers, and at one point some sixty members of the family were listed as thieves and robbers. They would steal anything. Cattle was a favourite quarry, but a reiver would be just as happy taking salmon from a rival's stream or kidnapping an enemy and holding him to ransom. The English warden, whose job it was to enforce what passed for law in the region, described the area as 'ungovernable' in 1579, by which time reiving had been a way of life for over a century.

But in 1606 things changed. England's new king, James I, was also James VI of Scotland. As monarch of both countries, James had no interest in border disputes or the lawlessness of the Debatable Land. So he ordered his men to break up the reivers, and some families, including the Grahams, were sent into exile in Ireland.

And there it might have ended if the Grahams had not had such a strong survival instinct. In fact, later family members returned to the area and to Brackenhill and lived here, more peacefully than before, for several generations. The fifth Richard Graham added to the building in around 1717, putting up brick cottages to the south-east of the tower. But otherwise the place changed little until the nineteenth century, by which time it had passed out of Graham hands.

The Spartan conditions in the tower were not to the taste of comfort-loving Victorians. In the 1860s the Standish family linked the tower and cottages to form a hunting lodge. The main living hall of the tower, originally a double-height room, was divided to make an extra storey. Today, the compact Victorian fireplace can be seen within the old Tudor one, which would have fitted much more naturally into the original tall hall. Otherwise, the Victorians did remarkably little to the tower, actually preserving many of its original features. We have them to thank that Brackenhill survives as a unique Scottish tower house in an English setting.

The thick walls of the tower have stood solid for over 400 years. But with a hole in the roof – and several holes in the floors and ceilings – the building is under threat from water and encroaching plant life. Already, the parapet at the top of the tower is leaning severely, and conservationists fear that the walls could finally start to crumble. Restored, the tower could form part of a heritage centre where visitors could learn about the history of the border region. So modern Grahams, and others who are gripped by the history of the borderlands, want to restore and protect the tower – before the weather does what generations of reivers could not.

The Victorian windows and other additions look out of place, but we should be thankful to their builders for helping to preserve Brackenhill Tower's structure.

Victoria Baths MANCHESTER

A palace of hygiene

ABOVE LEFT *Curvaceous scrollwork adorns the cast-iron structure of the changing stalls in the main pool at Victoria Baths.*

ABOVE RIGHT *When the baths first opened, men heading for the second-class pool paid only two old pence for entry. 'Males First Class', by contrast, paid six old pence.*

OPPOSITE *From the bottom of the pool to the top of the walls, the first-class pool is beautifully tiled. Art Nouveau iron railings line the balcony, giving a touch of richness to the decorative scheme.*

Victorian Manchester was a boom town, but its success came at a cost. Life was grim for ordinary people. Those in work could toil fourteen hours a day, seven days a week, for low wages. They breathed an atmosphere polluted by factories and railways, and influenza, pneumonia and asthma were rife. In some poor areas, a working man was lucky to reach the end of his teens. By the end of the nineteenth century the authorities realized that something had to be done.

By then, scientists were showing that hygiene was important for health. But as only one Manchester house in forty had running water, even keeping clean was a struggle. The answer was public baths, and Manchester's councillors decided that their city should have the best they could afford. The new city architect, Henry Price, was put in charge of the project, and the most amazing and lavish bath complex began to emerge above Manchester's rows of red-brick houses. As Ptolemy puts it, the baths represent 'municipal pride at its absolute best'.

From the outside, the baths are a dazzling composition of gables, chimneys and a clock tower – all in a combination of red brick and cream-coloured terracotta. The terracotta is used in stripes to contrast with the brick and is also seen in details around the windows and in signs above the entrances: 'Males first class', 'Males second class' and 'Females'. The terracotta helps the building stand out from the surrounding houses, yet the red brick blends with them. The style, with round-headed windows and moulded details, is nominally Renaissance, but no Renaissance building was quite like this: it is simply unique.

ABOVE LEFT *The bath's architect had a keen eye for detail. Even such small elements as the numbers above the changing stalls, set in their gently curving mounts, are carefully designed.*

ABOVE RIGHT *An iron framework supports a roof with a generous amount of glass, to let in plenty of natural light.*

Stepping into the entrance hall, one can see straight away that the building is as lavish inside. A wood and stained-glass ticket booth occupies one corner. There are Minton tiles everywhere – up the walls, along the stairwell, even covering the stair balusters and handrails. The baths are a world made of fine ceramics, a symbol of both luxury and cleanliness, of both health and art. A copper plaque commemorates the opening of the baths in 1906, and on the floor are mosaics portraying delightful cavorting fish. The whole decorative scheme is designed in the manner that was the height of fashion in the early 1900s – heavily influenced by the French style known as Art Nouveau. With its undulating curves and abstracted floral patterns, Art Nouveau dominated all the applied arts at this time, from metalwork to ceramics. It certainly left its mark here.

The actual facilities were just as sumptuous. There were three swimming pools, Turkish baths, Russian baths, over sixty individual slipper baths for people who needed to get clean, and a variety of other facilities including a drinking fountain and a shampooing room. These features and the class divisions reveal that this was not simply a place where the workers came for a wash. Victoria Baths is near the homes of both the working and middle classes; while the poor came for the slipper baths, the better off could enjoy a swim or an invigorating 'needle shower'. People paid sixpence for the privilege of swimming in the select first-class pool, but the 'second-class' males paid only tuppence, as they would at any other pool – this lower charge was fixed by an Act of Parliament.

The male first-class pool is the most extravagant in the complex. The cast-iron details are still all there, although now they are painted pale blue. Where the paint is peeling, a rainbow of earlier colours is revealed. Ptolemy suggests that the original may have been a deep green, to match the striped tiles that run all the way around this large space. Stained glass in windows high up in the walls is another high-quality decorative feature.

Also patronized by the wealthy, the Turkish baths share the rich decoration of the large men's pool. Once again the finish is of a high standard. Even the corners are covered with rounded tiles, except at the highest level, so that there are no sharp edges for the bathers to collide with as they move through the steamy atmosphere. Other areas of the complex, such as the slipper baths and the second-class pool, are plainer but still elegant and functional.

All these fine finishes cost money. The original estimate for building the baths was £57,000. When this was announced, there was an outcry, and the authorities called for revised figures. Building went ahead with a budget of £39,316, but this was soon exceeded. In the end, when the baths opened,

On the stairs and in the entrance hall nearly every surface is covered with tiles. Where in an earlier building there might have been carved decoration – for example, on the capitals and baluster shafts – the builders of the baths used ceramic reliefs to produce an effect of both richness and hygiene.

OPPOSITE *A Venetian window, with its curve-topped central section, adds to the sense of grandeur and decoration created by the tiles and ironwork.*

the price tag had grown to over £59,000. Once people started to use the baths, though, they thought that it was money well spent. There was an air of luxury about the place, and the buildings were a source of pride. What was more, careful planning and the incorporation of features such as the building's own freshwater wells and storage tanks meant that running costs were kept down. In the end, the people of Manchester got good value for their money. The baths became a valued local facility, serving everyone from the poorest user of the slipper baths to Sunny Lowry, the first British woman to swim the Channel, who practised here.

ABOVE LEFT *The tilework shows meticulous detailing, from the decorative panels to the curving corners – which are easier on the shoulder if you bump into them!*

ABOVE RIGHT *Even the ironwork on the gates and turnstiles is full of curves, reflecting the fashionable Art Nouveau style.*

Until you look closely, Victoria Baths seems to be a building in good repair. But many of the tiles are cracked and the damage is more than skin deep. Marianne explains that water has found its way into the ironwork behind the tiles, rusting and expanding the metal and thus cracking the tiles. The council had to close the baths in 1993 due to prohibitively high running costs. Many people protested then, and restoring the baths would return a treasured amenity to the area, with Turkish baths and at least one swimming pool available for public use. But the building has a wider significance, for few such complexes survive from this date and Manchester's baths are of national importance, too.

THE NORTH EAST

RESTORATION

Ravensworth Castle GATESHEAD

Harperley Prisoner-of-War Camp CROOK

Wentworth Castle Gardens STAINBOROUGH

'Ravensworth is so special because it's an enormous secret right on the edge of a densely populated conurbation and there are all sorts of plans to redevelop it so that those people can come in and use it.'

Kate Adie champions
RAVENSWORTH CASTLE

'When you walk inside Harperley's crude concrete huts the past comes alive in a magical way. Through its living connections with our parents and grandparents it tells us something important about our history and shows us how former enemies can become friends.'

Michael Wood champions
HARPERLEY PRISONER-OF-WAR
CAMP

The area to the east of the Pennines is a place of hills, moors and breathtaking vistas. It begins, in the south, with the lush fields and sandy beaches of south-east Yorkshire. As you go northwards, you cross the rolling Yorkshire Wolds to reach the Vale of Pickering, inland from Scarborough. Still further north are the more dramatic uplands of the North York Moors, a landscape of sandstone etched by glaciers and now covered with dry-stone-walled fields and rougher, steeper heath-clad areas. Beyond the moors and the industrial towns of Middlesbrough and Newcastle upon Tyne lie the Cheviot Hills and the Northumberland National Park, areas where you can be truly alone. The population is low and thinly spread, and the views of hill after hill lead the eye towards the even emptier landscape of Scotland.

Quiet and remote as it seems, the North East has often played a role at the forefront of history. Since the Romans, it has been border country. As well as the eastern section of Hadrian's Wall there is still plenty of evidence of other buildings put up by the Roman garrison. Chesters, by the North Tyne, has the well-preserved remains of a Roman cavalry fort, together with a bathhouse, the commandant's lodgings and various administrative buildings. Structures at nearby Corbridge include a series of granaries. At the far eastern end of Hadrian's Wall, at South Shields, is a fort where modern archaeologists have reconstructed one of the gates.

The Romans built in long-lasting stone, but many later builders did not have the army of labourers to quarry, transport and work this material. So in many parts of the North East, where stone is less plentiful, the usual material for humble buildings like houses is brick. Brick prevails especially in the farms and villages of the more low-lying area to the south of the region. Brownish-red walls and bright-red pantiled roofs can be seen everywhere in south-eastern Yorkshire and the Vale of York. Many of these houses are as old as the eighteenth century, and they have a solid, well-built character that suggests that this, for the most part, has been prosperous farming country for hundreds of years.

Further north, on the North York Moors, brick gives way to more plentiful stone. The local rock is Jurassic sandstone, which comes in a range of yellows and greys. Matched with pantiles on the roofs, it makes for attractive villages among the grass and heather of the moors. There are isolated farms of the same material, often with two-storey houses linked to a single-storey

ABOVE LEFT *Dark sandstone houses dominate Blanchland, Northumberland. Most of the buildings date from the mid-eighteenth century when the local landlord restored the village.*

ABOVE RIGHT *High on a hill overlooking Richmond in North Yorkshire, the town's castle has a large square twelfth-century keep surrounded by even earlier curtain walls to keep out attackers.*

barn. Stone field walls complete the picture of a unified landscape, with buildings and natural environment in harmony.

The combination of stone and bright-red pantiles can also often be seen in houses near the coast of County Durham, where the stone is a cream-coloured magnesian limestone. Elsewhere, builders adopted whatever local material was going: brown stone in the Cheviots, where it is matched with roofs of slate; more brown sandstone in the northern Pennines, with roof coverings of heavy slabs of sandstone; and dark-grey limestone walls roofed with pantiles along the coast. In some places, to add further to the changing range, stone walls are colourwashed, a tradition particularly strong in some of the coastal fishing towns. This variety of building materials ensures that one need not go far in the North East to find buildings of interest and beauty.

Many of these buildings are churches, and the North East has some of our oldest places of worship. This is because in the Saxon period the area was a strong centre of Christianity, home to the Venerable Bede, the Saxon historian of England's Church and people, and a base for missionaries such as St Aidan. One or two small Saxon churches, their tall stone walls pierced with only tiny windows, survive from this time, rare reminders of an era when most buildings were made of wood and disappeared centuries ago. Escomb, a tiny church in an old mining village near Bishop Auckland, is the most perfect example, and it is perhaps the oldest complete church in the country. It consists only of a tall narrow nave and a small chancel dating from the seventh century, together with a porch added some time later. Other Saxon churches in the area, such as Monkwearmouth near Sunderland, are less well preserved, although Monkwearmouth does have its original Saxon tower.

After the Normans replaced England's Saxon rulers, this area once more became an outpost to be defended. The invaders marked their progress, and

Durham Cathedral is at the very centre of the old city. The Normans began the building, and the vast interior is still mainly Norman. Slightly later masons added the twin western towers, with their rows of narrow pointed arches.

held on to their power, by building strong castles. Many of North Yorkshire's early fortifications, such as Richmond, Pickering and Helmsley Castles, were begun by the Normans and remained centres of royal power for much of the Middle Ages.

The Normans were also enthusiastic church-builders, and Durham Cathedral is perhaps their greatest masterpiece. Its vast bulk towers above the River Wear, a testimony to the might of the Norman Church and the skill of its builders in the eleventh and twelfth centuries. It is just as great a statement of Norman power as William the Conqueror's castles or the walls he built around towns and cities. Inside, rows of semicircular arches are held up by pillars carved in abstract designs that look almost modern – great sweeping chevrons and spirals that curve around pillars almost as wide as houses and twice as high. Semicircular arches top the pillars, creating a perfect example of the style known as Romanesque – but better proportioned than anything the Romans left behind in Britain.

York Minster is the region's other world-class cathedral. Its ornate west front and trio of tall fifteenth-century towers would have stood out over the houses of medieval York as they do over the shops today. The Minster was begun well after Durham, in 1220, in the pointed-arched Gothic style. Construction and modification continued on and off for about 250 years, by which time it had grown to become Britain's largest cathedral .The long period of construction meant that its building spanned a period of changing architectural fashions, so details, such as the design of windows and carved ornament, vary widely in different parts of the cathedral. The north transept, for example, is lit with the simple, narrow lancet windows popular in the early thirteenth century. But many other parts of the cathedral have the larger windows of the fourteenth and fifteenth centuries, with their filigree patterns of stone tracery.

Almost as spectacular is the cluster of north-eastern medieval monasteries built in the twelfth and thirteenth centuries. Many of these belonged to the Cistercians, an austere order who preferred isolated sites where they could farm and live in peace away from the tempting fleshpots of town and city. The quiet, isolated countryside of North Yorkshire, with its good sheep pasture, obviously appealed to the Cistercians, who left behind monasteries at Yorkshire sites such as Rievaulx, Jervaulx, Byland and Fountains. The latter, near Ripon, was at one time the largest and richest of all their houses, although now, like the others, it is an evocative ruin. The Cistercians developed an austere architectural style all their own, low on elaborate decoration but high on proportional flair. Their churches, with their forests of multi-shafted columns and severe, pointed arches, still lift the heart, although now when one looks up one sees not stained glass but trees, hills beyond and the vast expanse of the sky.

The Cistercian abbeys stand apart, ideally placed in this lonely, sparsely populated country. But the North East has its towns, as different in their style as industrial Newcastle, the well-to-do coastal town of Scarborough and medieval York. In addition to its cathedral, York indeed has much to offer anyone who wants to explore buildings. The medieval Clifford's Tower forms the shell of a thirteenth-century castle. There are still narrow winding medieval streets, old churches around every corner, and ancient city walls. Later periods are represented, too. The Assembly Rooms, with their rows of Corinthian columns, were designed by Lord Burlington, the leader of the Palladian movement in the eighteenth century.

The North East also has smaller places of character. The coastal town of Whitby has a ruined medieval abbey on the cliff facing the sea, and nearby is a church of the same period, full of eighteenth-century pews. The Old Town, a dense collection of mainly colourwashed red-roofed houses, is clustered around the harbour. Looking down at it from the cliffs by the church, one can see an intricate pattern of cobbled streets and pathways, the buildings jammed together to use every available space. Something of the same densely packed quality can be seen in other coastal towns, such as Robin Hood's Bay.

Scarborough prospered as a popular resort from the seventeenth century. Like many such towns, it began as a spa and went on to promote the new fashion of sea bathing in the eighteenth and nineteenth centuries. Bathing caught on, and Scarborough grew with streets of new houses and hotels above its towering cliffs. One of the town's most imposing buildings is the aptly named Grand Hotel,

A view of the old Yorkshire town of Whitby shows the restricted site between the sea and the steep cliff where the church punctuates the skyline. House builders had to make use of every available square foot of ground.

Three of Newcastle's fine bridges can be seen in this view from the riverside – the High Level Bridge, the 1920s Tyne Bridge and the low Swing Road Bridge.

designed in the 1860s by Cuthbert Brodrick, the architect of Leeds Town Hall. Towns like Whitby and Scarborough are just as typical of the area and just as absorbing in their way as the isolated farms and stone villages of the North York Moors. The North East is visually rich in both town and country.

Coal was a major source of work and wealth in County Durham and Northumberland. It fuelled the Industrial Revolution and brought different structures and building styles to the North East. The first railway to use steam locomotives ran between Stockton and Darlington. Rows of miners' cottages still provide homes for people. Pithead buildings and the vestiges of other heavy industries, such as steel production and lead mining, also survive.

The greatest of the working cities was Newcastle upon Tyne, which expanded as a result of a successful shipbuilding industry. Appropriately for a city founded on marine engineering, its progress can be charted via its famous collection of bridges over the river. The oldest, the High Level Bridge, was built by one of the fathers of the Industrial Revolution, engineer Robert Stephenson. It was begun in 1846 and is remarkable for carrying both road and rail traffic on separate levels. The bridge is beautiful as well as functional, a composition of cast-iron arches and columns. Nearby is the single low arch of the Swing Road Bridge, powered by locally made hydraulics that nudge the roadway to one side when shipping needs to pass. It was opened in 1876. Overlooking them both is the great Tyne Bridge of the 1920s, with its single, sweeping bowstring arch. Most of the later structures crossing the river are less striking, but the most recent, Wilkinson Eyre's Millennium Footbridge, with its twin curving white arches illuminated at night, is perhaps the most stunning of all the Tyne bridges.

Fishing, together with heavy industries such as mining and shipbuilding brought wealth to the North East, employing thousands in the towns of Northumberland and County Durham. But these businesses have declined now and high unemployment and urban dilapidation are the results in many towns. In many centres, such as Gateshead, regeneration schemes are helping some of the communities to recover. Flagship projects, such as the centre of performance and music education called the Sage, Gateshead, lead the way forward. The Sage's curving glazed contours throw light on to the river, making another dramatic landmark to complement the Tyne's famous bridges. The building will be followed by a cluster of apartment towers and various commercial developments. All these schemes are complemented by major restoration projects, which bring new uses for old buildings. One of the best known is the conversion of the huge Baltic Flour Mills in Gateshead into a major centre for contemporary visual arts. Such ambitious schemes are powerful signs of hope — both for the built environment and for the people who use it.

Ravensworth Castle GATESHEAD

The ruins of a businessman's fantasy castle

ABOVE LEFT *With its cluster of towers among the trees, Ravensworth still gives the impression of a romantic castle.*

ABOVE RIGHT *Before its decline, Ravensworth displayed all the trappings of an ancient castle, such as battlements, turrets and overhanging parapets. But its big, nineteenth-century windows gave the game away – it was really a luxurious country house.*

OPPOSITE *The flattened arches in the stable yard recall the buildings of the Tudor period, creating an impression rather like that of an Oxford or Cambridge college quad.*

Hidden among the trees a matter of minutes from the centre of Gateshead lies the most tantalizing ruin. A few sandstone towers, some lumps and bumps in the ground and a ruined stable block – this is all that remains of Ravensworth Castle. Today, few people know that Ravensworth exists, but it was once one of the greatest country houses of the North East.

Ravensworth reached the height of its fame in the nineteenth century. Its owner, Thomas Liddell, was a rich mine owner who decided to upgrade his home. There had been a castle at Ravensworth since at least the fourteenth century, and the Liddells had built themselves a large, plain Georgian house here in the 1720s. But Thomas wanted something grander. He was a friend of the Prince Regent, so naturally he turned to the prince's architect, John Nash, the designer of Brighton's Royal Pavilion and the terraces around London's Regent's Park. Nash came up with a massive fantasy castle. There were at least twelve towers and turrets, battlemented walls, pointed arches and rows of mullioned windows. Inside, many rooms had vaulted ceilings and panelled walls. There was an enormous great hall with a row of nine tall Gothic windows, a high hammer-beam roof, a double staircase and a minstrels' gallery. For Nash, who designed many country houses, it was one of his most ambitious projects. But it seems that his clients also lent a hand – one nineteenth-century account says that the main front of the house was designed by the Hon. H. T. Liddell, son of the owner.

The house survived until the 1950s. By this time the expense of running and maintaining the large house was colossal and death duties put an extra burden on the family. As a result of these pressures, hundreds of country houses were pulled down in the 1950s as their owners realized they would never be able to afford the expense of running them, let alone the cost of the endless round of repairs needed in any old building. At Ravensworth there was a further problem – the house was slowly collapsing as a result of subsidence. With a crushing irony for a house built with the profits of coal, the subsidence was caused by mine workings underneath the building. So the Liddells left, and most of the house was demolished. The stone reused for other buildings, including three nearby cottages.

The ruin that survives presents a fascinating glimpse of the history of the house. One octagonal Gothic tower remains from the grand front designed by Nash and Liddell. Although in a ruinous state, the tower preserves many of the Gothic features that would have been seen all over the house: the pointed and mullioned windows, the ranks of shafts on either side of the doorway, the stone-vaulted ceiling of the entrance passage. To the north and west of the tower, mounds of rubble and bumps in the ground mark the walls of the once-great house.

There is little else of the house itself, but much more remains of its large stable block. Here, many of the walls are still standing, although they are in poor repair and open to the sky. The buildings of the stable block form a square courtyard, including two ranges of single-storey stables, an octagonal clock tower, some cottages and a three-storey gatehouse. Making, in

ABOVE LEFT *Turned finials survive amongst the decaying woodwork of the stable stalls.*

ABOVE CENTRE *A small tower protrudes above a doorway in one corner of the yard. Again, the buildings display a hybrid style – the tower's pointed arches look gothic, but the large windows below could come from a Tudor or Jacobean building.*

ABOVE RIGHT *Some leaded panes remain to show future restorers how the windows were glazed.*

OPPOSITE *The stable yard is an eccentric collection of real medieval towers, nineteenth-century imitations and connecting curtain walls.*

Ptolemy's words, 'a whole township of ruins', these buildings are in the same Gothic style as the main house and are sound enough to be restored.

The stable complex is especially interesting because it contains, as well as the work by Nash, two fragments of the original medieval Ravensworth Castle: a pair of genuine Gothic towers to complement Nash's Gothic-revival buildings. The architecture of these ancient towers is rather different from their nineteenth-century equivalents. The stonework is much more massive, with thick walls and big blocks of stone. As Marianne observes, there is little in the way of decoration: the fireplaces are very simple in design, and the ceilings are the plainest stone barrel vaults with no ribs or carved bosses. The windows are small, and there is no symmetry about their arrangement – the builders of the old towers just put a window in where they needed one, with little thought of outside appearance.

So although the Victorian house and the ancient towers are both built in the Gothic style, there is a world of difference: the medieval towers are strong and utilitarian, the nineteenth-century work built very much with appearance in mind. So why did Liddell and Nash keep the ancient towers? One reason may have been to create a link between the Liddell family and the ancient lords of the North East. The Liddells had become rich through trade, but they probably wanted to associate themselves with the old landed families of the area. They made the link obvious by leaving their stable block, with its ancient towers, in full view of the carriage drive leading to the house – the block was not tucked away around the back as such stable blocks were in most nineteenth-century houses, and the old towers could be seen clearly by visitors.

Ravensworth impressed the scores of guests who came to parties here in the nineteenth century. It also won a place in the hearts of local people who came to watch the lavish military tattoos staged here in the early years of the twentieth. Architectural experts were impressed, too. Nikolaus Pevsner, who was writing the volume on County Durham in his *Buildings of England* series as the house was being demolished, called it 'the most splendid and the most picturesque monument of the romantic medieval revival in the country'. The place is now a romantic ruin, and it would be impossible to rebuild the main castle as it was in Thomas Liddell's time. But the fragments could be stabilized and made safe so that visitors could enjoy them and go on heritage or nature trails nearby. And the stable complex could be restored and put to good use. Space here may be used by Great North Forest, an organization that will provide training in forestry and will open up the surrounding land to public access. Once more, people would be able to come to Ravensworth, marvel at the vision of Nash and Liddell and admire the work of the medieval masons who went before them.

Harperley Prisoner-of-War Camp CROOK

An evocative reminder of the Second World War

ABOVE LEFT *The huts of the camp are arranged in rows, following the contours of a gentle slope. These buildings show a mixture of materials, including concrete blocks and posts, bricks, wood, and corrugated iron.*

ABOVE RIGHT *Parts of the walls are covered with terracotta-coloured facing tiles.*

OPPOSITE *This detail of one of the huts shows a doorway that no longer has a door, exposing the interior to the elements.*

From the outside, Harperley Prisoner-of-War Camp in County Durham looks like a collection of old huts – and leaky, badly built huts at that. But it is much more than this. It is an unusual survivor that played a special part in British history in the dark days of the Second World War and for some years afterwards. It is proof that interesting old buildings do not have to be grand or monumental – what is important is the human story they tell.

Harperley was built in 1942. It was one of around 1,500 prisoner-of-war camps in Britain, all but a handful of which have been demolished. The first prisoners to arrive at the eight-acre site were Italians. To begin with, they helped to build the huts, sleeping in tents at night until the buildings were completed in January 1943. After a few months, the Italians were dispersed to various hostels and farms in the area. The camp then filled up with a new intake, conscripts from the German army who were designated as 'low risk' and were allowed to do essential work on farms and construction sites, returning to the camp in the evenings. They could earn up to six shillings a week, and some supplemented this by carving toys or making other items that they sold locally.

The German prisoners stayed at the camp until they were allowed to return home in the years after 1945. By the summer of 1948, the last prisoners had left, and the camp buildings were taken over for agricultural use – for storage, as poultry sheds and by a market garden. Finally, they were left to the encroaching moss and brambles.

Many prisoner-of-war camps were made of timber, like traditional garden sheds. But a number of the buildings at Harperley followed a design and construction technique that was new in the early 1940s. This involved using prefabricated concrete panels. First of all, brick plinths were built to act as bases for the walls. The builders poured concrete into the areas between the plinths to form the floor and erected concrete posts at the corners and at regular intervals along each side of the building. These posts were formed with a vertical groove running along each side, and flat concrete panels were simply slid into the grooves to build up the walls. Finally, the gaps between the panels were sealed with bitumen to make the walls waterproof.

The crude construction of the buildings reminds the visitor that no one cared much for appearances when the huts were built. The important thing was to get the buildings up as quickly as possible.

This sort of building could be erected at speed and so was ideal for wartime, when the number of prisoners was increasing rapidly. The components did not have to be of high quality, and, as Ptolemy notes, there is every sign that the concrete for the panels, which is full of air bubbles, was poured quickly by unskilled labour. But the huts were utilitarian buildings designed to last only a few years, so quality of finish was hardly important.

As it turns out, they have lasted sixty years. The structures are surprisingly sound, although there are problems. One of these goes to the heart of the upright posts that hold the buildings together. These uprights are made from reinforced concrete – concrete strengthened with steel rods that pass right through the inside of each post. Moisture and air have penetrated the concrete, causing the steel to rust and expand, in turn making the concrete break up. If corrective measures are not taken, some of the posts will collapse, taking the buildings with them.

Harperley had to be a self-contained complex. The 1,000 or so prisoners were looked after in the camp's own healthcare facilities, with a doctor and dentist working on-site. There were educational courses, which were useful for young men whose schooling had been interrupted by the war.

ABOVE LEFT *In the camp theatre, ceiling panels and windowpanes are broken, but the interior is in remarkably good condition. This view looks down the raked floor towards the small stage and orchestra pit.*

ABOVE RIGHT *Some of the murals in the mess hall show the unknown artist's skill at painting animals.*

Outside, there was a sports field, on which prisoners played against football teams from nearby camps and villages. There was even a chapel, decorated by the prisoners and supplied with its own priest.

One of the most surprising facilities in the camp was the hut that was converted into a theatre. Many of the fittings still survive: a small stage, with prompt box and orchestra pit for the prisoners' eleven-piece band, and the floor of the auditorium, which is built up in steps for seating. There are still traces of the decoration – red and yellow panels on both walls and ceiling to give a feeling of richness in imitation of the more ornamental theatres in the outside world. The special electric lighting has long since disappeared, although traces of its wiring remain. Decorative papier-mâché theatrical masks have also gone from the panel above the stage. But an atmosphere of entertainment and relaxation survives, and former inmates remember the shows put on by the camp's theatre group, under its leader and resident composer Helmut Enz.

The theatre reveals how the prisoners at Harperley were determined to make the best of things, to have a good time in spite of the fact that they were confined in an alien country far from their own land. The same spirit can be seen in the mess hall. This is beautifully decorated with paintings of horses, deer, goatherds wearing lederhosen, and other idealized scenes from German rural life. The artist is unknown, but his work has transformed the interior of the dour hut. The illusion is completed by the trompe l'oeil 'curtains' made of painted hardboard that still adorn the windows, an effect Ptolemy describes as 'Hansel and Gretel in hardboard'. The whole decorative scheme was no doubt intended to make the surroundings seem a little bit more like home.

Currently, very few British prisoner-of-war camps can be visited by the public. Clearly, there is scope for another to be opened, especially one with the unique features of Harperley. The theatre, canteen, reception area and other parts of the camp could be fully restored, and other huts could be used for displays on Harperley's history, on different aspects of life there and on the local home front during the Second World War. It could be a fascinating window on to our more recent history.

Wentworth Castle Gardens STAINBOROUGH

Garden buildings to amaze the neighbours

The fragile, narrow glazing bars of the conservatory at Wentworth make it impossible to climb on top of the building, something that has made repairs to the roofs very difficult.

OPPOSITE *In spite of the broken glass there is enough heat and shelter inside the conservatory to ensure that many of the old plants are still thriving.*

Rivalry can be a spur to achievement. In 1695 William Wentworth, second Earl of Strafford, died childless. His next of kin, Thomas Wentworth, expected to inherit the family estate at Wentworth Woodhouse, but instead William left it to another relative, Thomas Watson. Thomas Wentworth, angry at being cut off, hit back. He bought a nearby estate at Stainborough, near Barnsley, and set about upgrading the house and grounds in the hope of producing an effect grander and more amazing than anything his rivals possessed. It was the start of a campaign of building and garden improvements that went on through the eighteenth and nineteenth centuries.

Thomas's house, Wentworth Castle, is at the heart of a large landscape garden containing more than two dozen buildings and ornamental structures. They include temples, monuments, towers and follies that act as focal points to vistas as one walks through the garden. Together with the landscape itself, they make up one of the most notable gardens in northern England. Two structures are especially notable and at particular risk: the conservatory near the house and Stainborough Castle, an enormous folly on a rise to the west, about half a mile away.

OPPOSITE *Wentworth's sham castle has a gatehouse flanked by round towers. It looks medieval from a distance, although details such as the large ornate stones around the central arch give the game away.*

The castle came first. Thomas probably began it in 1727, and it was substantially finished three years later. It is as large as many genuine castles and stands proud, if ruinous, at the top of a hill, which was an earthwork centuries before Thomas's time, perhaps as long ago as the Saxon period. So Wentworth may have been building his sham castle where a real one had stood in the Middle Ages.

This view of one of the castle's square towers, surrounded by invasive trees and weeds, shows clearly the decorative windows on the upper floor.

Thomas's castle is square in plan, with four square towers on the walls. There is also a huge gatehouse, which originally had four round corner towers, although two of these fell down during a storm in 1962. Thomas obviously had a special affection for these towers – he named three of them after his three daughters. He was also making a statement. He might have been deprived of his rightful title and inheritance, but this ruin, in the ancient style, showed that he was a member of an 'old' family.

The castle certainly looks impressive, but it is very much an eighteenth-century idea of a medieval fortress. The square towers have quite large windows shaped as ornamental quatrefoils, rather than the narrow arrow slits preferred by medieval knights. Inside the towers, the walls are plastered and painted. There were obviously comfortable rooms here, from which the family could admire the view, although the floors and roofs have long since disappeared.

A closer look at the structure shows that it is far from strong and solid. The castle was built of local sandstone, and Marianne notes how erosion has worn away the stone completely in many places, leaving large pits where there were once hefty chunks of masonry. Subsidence has made the structure still weaker.

Thomas was one of the first people in Britain to construct a sham castle, a form of building that was later to become very popular on English country estates. He was one of the trendsetters in the movement to revive the Gothic style of architecture that was soon to take root. It would be sad to see his epoch-making building continue to crumble away.

Wentworth's conservatory was built in the 1840s by Frederick Vernon-Wentworth. At this time, such structures were the height of fashion. British explorers were travelling the world and bringing back specimens of exotic plant species unknown in Europe. Many of these plants could survive only in hot conditions, so heated greenhouses and conservatories became the rage.

Many of the conservatory's details, such as these cast-iron panels at the tops of the glass 'walls', are exquisite. Their spiralling, foliage-like decoration is designed to mirror the growth of the plants inside.

The entrance to the conservatory is topped with a shallow triangular pediment – a hint of grandeur amongst the rust and missing panes of glass.

Already fashionable in the late eighteenth century, hothouses were given a boost in the nineteenth century because engineers developed the use of cast iron, an ideal material for the narrow columns and glazing bars needed in such buildings. The great Palm House at Kew Gardens led the way in the mid-1840s, and the Wentworth conservatory was part of the same greenhouse-building boom.

The conservatory is beautiful but fragile. The main structure is made of glass supported by slender cast-iron columns, beams and glazing bars. This delicate network of glass walls and roofs sits on a low stone plinth. On the south side is a projecting porch, also of iron and glass, which is the main entrance. There is also a bridge, added later, which links the conservatory to the main house.

The building was strong on technology. Rainwater was collected from the pitched roofs and fed into the hollow cast-iron columns, which took it to underground storage tanks. Under iron grilles in the floor are heating pipes that kept the hothouse up to temperature. The glazing bars are as thin as possible, to let in the maximum amount of light. Ptolemy, while admiring these innovative features, recognizes that they have also contributed to the building's decay. The all-glass construction means that it is very difficult to get on to the roof to repair broken panes. Blockages in the clever hollow columns have led to seepage of water and rust, and many of the uprights need replacing completely. Structural movement has added to the problems, causing cracks and weaknesses in the stone plinths – a problem exacerbated by water leaks. As a result of all this damage, the conservatory is very frail indeed. But it could be saved, and should be, for it is an outstanding example of an early glass and iron structure of its type.

Wentworth's Castle and its estate survived until the Second World War. Like many country houses, it was used during the war by the military and after 1945 the family sold the house and pleasure grounds. Since then, many buildings fell into decay but today, with buildings and park in public ownership, there is more hope than ever that the castle and conservatory will be saved. The sham castle needs to be stabilized to make the structure safe, but it could then continue to give pleasure as a romantic ruin and perhaps as a backdrop for theatrical productions. The conservatory, when restored, could once more delight visitors and become a fitting home for the many mature plants still surviving defiantly inside.

WALES

RESTORATION

Faenol Old Hall BANGOR
Amlwch Port and Parys Mountain ANGLESEY
Llanelly House LLANELLI

'Faenol is a wonderfully solid, tough house that holds its secrets from you until it feels you're worth learning them. The idea that this splendid old house should provide a living classroom for today's master craftsmen, that is thrilling.'

Robert Hardy champions
FAENOL OLD HALL

'Anglesey was the greatest exporter of copper in the world and one of the busiest ports in the United Kingdom. It needs to be restored and made accessible to create a vitality that the area needs.'

Glenys Kinnock champions
AMLWCH AND PARYS MOUNTAIN

'Llanelly House is so peculiar, it needs preservation simply because of its rarity. It's one of those rather quirky buildings that the British have always done so well, where all the styles that we have are reflected in one space.'

Laurence Llewelyn-Bowen
champions LLANELLY HOUSE

Crossing from England, once the traveller is through the marcher or border country, there is no mistaking the separateness of Wales. In the north is some of Britain's most breathtaking scenery, mountains and hills dominated by Snowdon and spreading from the Lleyn Peninsula in the west to the borders with Cheshire in the east. Elsewhere, the lonely, rolling fields of mid-Wales give way to the more populous south. Here, the cities of Cardiff and Swansea and the old coal towns of the valleys had a magnetic pull for the population as men came to find jobs in the mines and steelworks. But the south is far from exclusively urban. It is also the location of the beauties of the Gower Peninsula and far western Pembrokeshire, and the open uplands of the Brecon Beacons. In some parts of rural Wales, such as the Beacons or Snowdonia, you can travel for miles without seeing a building, and when you do it is an isolated farm – villages are thin on the ground here. But Wales has its own unique styles of building, and in some places the traditions go back thousands of years.

From the prehistoric sites of Pembrokeshire in the south-west to the huge concentration of burial mounds and ring ditches in the north-east, there is plenty of evidence of the native prehistoric people of Wales. But in terms of buildings, the most notable early remains are evidence of the tensions between Wales and England. In Roman times, this was frontier country, a place of forts like Caerleon, where the foundations of the barrack blocks and the remarkable amphitheatre are still visible. Later, there were the disputes and demarcations marked by Offa's Dyke, the famous boundary dug by the king of the Saxon kingdom of Mercia. In the Middle Ages, Wales was fought over by the English, and many of the surviving medieval buildings tell the tale of this struggle. Later, with the coming of industry in the eighteenth century, Wales – especially south Wales – played a major part in fuelling the change. Coal mining and ironworking transformed the landscape of this part of the country, and although now gone these industries have left their marks behind them. And so, with a unique blend of industrial and rural culture, Wales offers a rich built environment – and much scope for the restorer.

Wales covers a large area, its variety of scenery underpinned with many different rocks. Even so, there is a unifying pattern to the traditional buildings of rural Wales, from the isolated farms and barns that dot the landscape of much of mid-Wales to the villages of the Vale of Glamorgan in the south. Most

At Corris, a cluster of buildings, covered in roofs of Welsh slate, clings to the hillside. It is a pattern of settlement and architecture common in many small towns in Wales.

of the local rocks are dark, but many of the houses are whitewashed and small, their low walls covered with roofs of local slate. The whitewash is especially common along the coast, as in other parts of Britain, and is applied over all sorts of materials, from stone to brick. This, and the ubiquitous slate roofs, gives a unity both to rural landscapes and the streets of coastal towns.

In the southern towns, where mining dominated the economy in the nineteenth and twentieth centuries, row upon row of cottages were built for the workers. These were small houses in long terraces stretching up the sides of valleys. To begin with they were often built of dark sandstone, but later they were more likely to be of brick. They could look dour, but in places the brick is in two colours, laid in striped courses, or the walls are painted over in brilliant colours so that they look more bright and cheerful. Many of these cottages remain, though the mines have long closed.

Blue-grey Welsh slates were used all over Britain in the nineteenth and twentieth centuries. They made strong, lightweight, easily built roofs that could last for a century, and they were taken up everywhere. And so Wales played its part in the enormous expansion of Victorian towns and cities, with their streets of red-brick, slate-roofed houses, from tiny back-to-back terraces to grand detached villas. Millions of these slates – thin, smooth and perfectly straight – can be seen in Wales itself. But others – thicker, rougher and with more rounded corners – were produced for local use. These more 'rustic' slates give a roof the softer, less machine-finished look still seen on some rural Welsh houses and farm buildings.

Slate is a superb roofing material. It splits easily into thin sheets, which means that a covering of slates does not weigh as much as a tile or stone roof and so does not need massive timbers to support it. It is also waterproof: laid in regular, overlapping courses, it is all that is needed to keep a house dry.

But in some places roofers used joints of lime mortar between the slates to stop heavy, driving rain from getting blown in through the gaps. Sometimes the entire roof could be covered in a pale mortar slurry for added protection. But on the whole the grey of untreated slates is the dominant roof colour.

In the east, towards the border with England, the pattern of building changes. As in the English counties of Shropshire and Herefordshire, this was a country of trees, and there are many timber-framed, black and white houses – but with a difference. Whereas in England they are roofed with thatch or tiles, in Wales they are more likely to be covered with Welsh slates.

Welsh stone and slate were also used to build some of the area's most famous buildings: its castles. Most striking of all is the group of English castles in the north, built by Edward I in his campaign to conquer and rule the Welsh. Distributed around the north Welsh coast, Caernarfon, Conwy, Harlech and Beaumaris are Britain's most outstanding medieval fortifications, and there are several other castles, almost equally striking, in the region. Their walls – tall, thick and overlooked by multiple towers – are obviously strong, and a closer look reveals a host of other details built in to make them well-nigh impregnable. Arrow loops and crenellations enable the inhabitants to fire on attackers. Holes are provided through which the garrison could discharge boiling oil or drop missiles on to enemies below. Walls at different heights allow defenders to rain out arrows at several levels at once. Gatehouses with multiple drawbridges and portcullises keep the enemy out. This is the architecture of the oppressor, but no less impressive for that.

The polygonal towers and tall curtain walls of Caenarfon Castle are some of the largest of any British castle. It was built by Edward I as his main headquarters in Wales and its walls of limestone striped with darker bands of sandstone recall the walls of the great city of Constantinople, which the king would have seen during the crusades.

The Welsh built their own castles, too. These tend to be smaller than the English ones, but are still strong and imposing. Criccieth and Dolbadarn, on the Lleyn Peninsula, are two of the best. There are also outstanding castles further south, built and manned by English lords charged with keeping order and defending the borders. Caerphilly, now set among the industrial towns of the south, is the biggest of them all, defended by a complex of moats and lakes that cover no fewer than thirty acres.

Wales is not as well known for its country houses as it is for its castles, but there are many large houses from every period from Tudor to Victorian. Erddig, near Wrexham, is one of the most famous. It retains many rare furnishings and other features from the eighteenth century, including beautiful Chinese wallpaper. But its true glory is the huge range of service buildings, from kitchen and laundry to sawmill and smithy, together with the unique records of the servants who worked there.

Some of the later great houses were, if anything, more lavish, as wealth from coal and industry funded a new boom in domestic architecture. One result of this was a revival of castle architecture in Wales. In the nineteenth century, the Marquess of Bute, rich from the ownership of mining rights throughout south Wales, employed architect William Burges to restore Cardiff Castle. The result is a fantastic collection of towers and turrets, pointed roofs and wooden hoardings, which brings a fanciful, fairy-tale atmosphere to Cardiff's workaday skyline. The interior is even more fanciful, with suites of rooms decorated with tiles, rich paintwork, ornate woodwork and gilding in a range of styles from medieval to Moorish.

The people who lived in these buildings made up a long-established Christian community, for the faith came early to Wales. In the mid-sixth century, St David set up his monastery in western Pembrokeshire, and the settlement that grew up around it became the small city that still bears his name. The present buildings were put up long after David's time. The cathedral was begun in the twelfth century, and the large bishop's palace next door (now in ruins) was built between 1280 and 1350. But they are still evocative of this stronghold of one of the founders of Celtic Christianity.

The Normans built fine churches in Wales, at regional centres and market towns such as Carmarthen and Brecon. These are beautiful buildings, with their round arches and decorative carving, but the plainer, smaller country churches are more typical of Wales. These are usually built of rough stone or rubble and they are long and low, blending into the upland landscape. If there is a tower or bell turret, it, too, is low, and often there is no visible outside break between the nave and chancel. The appearance of these buildings has been described as like a long cottage with a large chimney at one end.

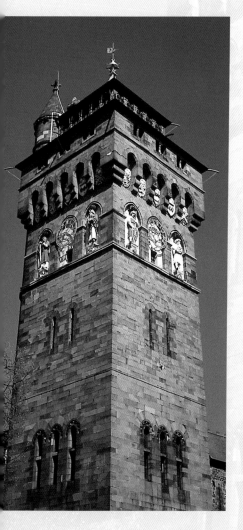

The main tower of Cardiff Castle was designed by architect William Burges in a kind of late-medieval Italian style, as if he was comparing his client, the Marquis of Bute, to one of the great princes of the Renaissance.

Religious dissent took a firm hold in Wales, and another characteristic building is the Nonconformist chapel. Small, with a plain pitched roof of slate, walls of brick or local stone, and a few round-headed windows, these modest buildings popped up everywhere in the nineteenth century. Many such chapels still stand, often put to new uses as shops or houses.

Wales has a long industrial heritage. Ironworkers were extracting ore in the Forest of Dean, on the borders of Wales and England, at least 2,000 years ago. But the boom came in the eighteenth century, and some buildings, like those at the fortress-like Blaenavon Ironworks, beneath the Coity Mountains in south Wales, remain to tell its story. There are preserved coal mines, too, with their winding gear and engine houses stark against the skyline and their surrounding terraces of cottages. Ironworking and coal mining were a perfect match for the industrialists of the nineteenth century – they used coke in the blast furnaces to smelt the iron, so one industry fuelled the other. But Welsh coal was used much more widely. Sent around the country on the trains it also fuelled, it powered machinery and heated houses everywhere.

We think of south Wales as the part of the principality with an industrial heritage, but the rest of Wales had its industries, too. Mills with water wheels processed the wool from the backs of the local sheep in mid- and north Wales. Some mills are still weaving cloth, their water-powered looms replaced with electric machinery. And among the picture-postcard scenery of the Snowdonia National Park are quarries where millions of tons of Welsh slate have been extracted. The enormous quarry at Dinorwig, with its grey, slate-roofed buildings, is now a museum of Welsh slate.

The old industries have declined now, but these traces remain, along with the houses of industrialists and their workers. Monuments like Cardiff Castle are at the heart of a city renewing itself with other, less extravagant buildings, such as the Millennium Stadium and the developments in the bay area. The castle, meanwhile, is in the custodianship of the city, a pointer to the way in which care for old buildings can foster local pride.

Faenol Old Hall BANGOR

History in stone

A replaced upper window contrasts with the earlier openings, their stone mullions still intact, on the lower floors of Faenol Old Hall.

OPPOSITE *Many parts of the interior have been taken back to the bare wood and stone, providing an opportunity to see how the floors, walls and roof structure have been put together.*

Dark walls, roughly shaped stones, a roof of slate – the Old Hall at Faenol, near the Menai Strait in Gwynedd, could only be in Wales. Yet, as Ptolemy points out, this is a much grander house than most in the principality, and its E-shaped plan and mullioned windows give it the air of a typical Tudor manor house. So there is something unusual about this building, a history waiting to be unravelled.

Faenol Old Hall was built, probably in the late 1570s, by Thomas Wyn ap William, generally known as Thomas Williams. Part of an important north Welsh landowning family, Thomas amassed a large estate around Faenol – partly by an advantageous marriage, partly by shady dealing – and built his home on the site of an earlier, probably medieval, house. Future generations of his family were just as successful. His son William bought himself a baronetcy and served as High Sheriff of his shire. Sir Thomas, the second baronet, was a justice of the peace and also High Sheriff. Another William fought his way through the Civil War, moving sides as the fortunes of king and Parliament changed. Meanwhile, the family was building up an estate of over 25,000 acres, much of which was rich in slate.

The Williams family did well, but it was the Assheton Smiths, who owned the estate from the eighteenth to the twentieth centuries, who made most money from the slate. This was because Welsh slate became the roofing material of choice in the building boom of the Victorian period, when millions of houses all over Britain were put up for the rapidly growing population. The Assheton Smiths were rich enough to build a new hall in the fashionable classical style some distance away, and the old house was left in the hands of farming tenants. Little altered for over 200 years, it remains a beautiful example of Tudor and Jacobean architecture.

Like most houses of its age, Faenol Old Hall developed over the years, its owners adapting it to changing standards of comfort and fashion. It probably started life as a hall house – a building with a single main living room, the hall, open from the ground floor to the roof. As time went by, people began to demand more comfort and privacy, so the hall was divided up, both vertically and horizontally, and extra wings were added, too. On the ground floor, there would have been a large 'public' room, where the lord would receive tenants, give orders to servants and do business. Upstairs were the private rooms,

ABOVE LEFT *Exposed panels of basketwork wattle reveal how they slot into the timber uprights. Thin, tough, flexible lengths of hazel were the favourite material for this technique.*

ABOVE CENTRE *This room is covered with oak moved from upstairs. The give-away is the varying sizes of the individual panels on the right-hand wall, where they have been cut to fit.*

ABOVE RIGHT *A forest of woodwork holds the roof together at a point where two gables meet. The undersides of the slates can be seen through the timbers.*

where the family spent most of its time and where guests were entertained. Later still, when it became fashionable to live on the ground floor and sleep upstairs, the functions of the rooms, and some of their decoration, changed once more. These alterations can be made out in the fabric of the house.

Even at a glance, some of the development of the house can be seen from the outside. At the front are three gables, but the right-hand one is different, its stepped profile suggesting a later date than the rest of the building. So the rooms in this wing were probably added during the seventeenth century.

You enter the house through its old door, still hanging on a pair of early iron hinges. The main downstairs room is an evocative, oak-panelled space topped with Tudor beams. But the panelling did not start out here. A close look shows that it has been cobbled together to fit the room and has been moved from elsewhere – probably from an upstairs room when the change from upper to lower reception rooms took place.

On the upper floor – reached by a fine seventeenth-century staircase – more of the house's history can be deduced. With many of the structural timbers revealed, it can be seen how, quite early in the building's lifetime, the framework was altered. This was probably done when the hall was divided up into smaller rooms. Downstairs, in the cellar, is evidence of an earlier phase, the original medieval house that Thomas Williams swept away to begin the building we see above ground today. So, as we look around the house, the history of the building begins to emerge: the medieval house, Thomas Williams's hall, and two further alterations during the seventeenth century. The building is an object lesson in architectural evolution.

And there are other clues to be followed. Today, much of Faenol Old Hall is structurally naked – much plaster and other decoration has disappeared, revealing the materials beneath. Panels of wattle – the basket-weave material of wooden staves and withies – can be viewed in the spaces between the oak framework. The joints used by the carpenters to hold the frame together

are often visible, as are the oak pegs used to hold them in place. The wooden structure that supports the roof can also be seen. Such details help one to grasp very quickly how the building was put together.

The Faenol Building Conservation Centre was established on the estate in 2000. Many students are already taking courses in such subjects as plastering and stonemasonry, and it is hoped to use the Old Hall to extend the centre's work by helping students and visitors to learn about the old constructional crafts. Many of the building's revealing details will therefore be left bare, to show how they were constructed. But there is much to do before this can be achieved. The house has been in slow decline ever since the family moved to their new hall. In places at the back of the house, the old walls have been altered to take inappropriate new metal window frames. Marianne stresses that this is the opposite of correct conservation practice, which always aims to fit the new to the old fabric. Numerous other details, from poor modern plaster to a polystyrene fireplace, will have to be removed. Modern cement has been used instead of lime mortar for pointing the stone walls, which is especially damaging, because soft lime mortar acts as an escape route for moisture. When this route is blocked by cement, the moisture has to come out through the stone, instigating a process of decay. Problems like this make action urgent, so that the walls of the house remain solid, protecting the wonderful details, from the beams and door of ancient oak to the mullioned windows, which give the house its character.

The porch and the left-hand wing are the main remains of the original house.

Amlwch Port and Parys Mountain ANGLESEY

A monument to an entire industry

ABOVE LEFT *The tall, well built harbour wall at Amlwch hints at a deep harbour where large boats could put in and fill up with a cargo of heavy copper ore.*

ABOVE RIGHT *Parys Mountain is a huge site at which the landscape has been transformed by centuries of copper mining. The resulting rock shapes have a weird beauty of their own.*

OPPOSITE *The old windmill is one of the few landmarks on the mountainside that can be seen from far away.*

The port of Amlwch, on Anglesey, is picturesque and popular with visitors. Its stone harbour walls, with their striking long stones laid vertically, enclose deep wharves that once welcomed large, ocean-going ships. Its architecture is reminiscent of Cornwall, but this was no fishing village. During the eighteenth and nineteenth centuries it was the centre of the trade in one of the most widely used and important metals – copper.

The signs of industrial activity are still here, with great stone copper bins, one still with its slate roof, evidence of the size of the business. Other buildings are testimony to the importance of shipping, for some of the finest sailing vessels of the period were built at Amlwch. A sail loft from around 1880 (now adapted as a heritage centre) preserves its sloping floor, designed to make it easier to unroll large bolts of canvas. And the Watch House, a building that combines offices and a lighthouse, still acts as a focus for the entire harbour area.

There is also a limekiln, built into the side of the hill. Limekilns were used to produce quicklime, a material used widely in the construction industry. It was made by mixing coal and limestone and heating them to a high temperature. The kiln's hillside location meant that it could be charged easily, cartloads of coal and limestone tipped in through a large circular opening at the top. The kiln was then fired to a temperature of around 900°C, and the quicklime flowed out of a small opening at the bottom. Mixed with aggregate and sand to form a lime render, it can be seen today on nearby buildings.

The top of the lime kiln at Amlwch is lined with stepped courses of bricks, to stop the edge caving in and to protect workers when they were tipping in the limestone.

If Amlwch has many remains of past industry, nearby Parys Mountain presents industrial history on a grand scale. Ptolemy describes it as a landscape out of science fiction, like a planetary surface of purple, green and grey rocks. The stone has been hacked away into stark hills and dips and a vast central hole filled with water to form a tarn. In the middle of all this, the tower of an abandoned windmill is one of the few signs of building activity. The whole landscape is what was left after the huge copper-mining industry declined in the late nineteenth century. Copper has been extracted from these rocks since the Bronze Age.

The discovery that Parys was worked in the Bronze Age gives the site an importance in the technological change that swept Europe when people first began to use metal to make tools and weapons some 4,000 years ago. Copper-workers were prepared to go to great lengths to extract this material, and some of their narrow tunnels into the rocks can still be seen. Here, they lit fires and threw water on to the rocks to make them crack. Then they pounded the lumps of ore with hammer stones to make more manageable pieces before smelting them to get the metal out. With this precious material they could make light, sharp axes and swords that transformed people's lives. Bronze, a mixture of copper and tin, was a key product for hundreds of years.

But the heyday of the Parys mines came much later, in the eighteenth century. In 1768 a miner called Rowland Puw discovered a huge, rich deposit of copper ore at Parys. People suddenly realized that the mountain was a source of untold wealth. Landowners vied for mining rights, and the man who came out on top was a local lawyer called Thomas Williams. He was soon controlling the whole mining operation, putting up warehouses, offices, kilns and smelters on the mountain and at Amlwch, and making a vast amount of money. He pushed his workers hard. Many of them were women and children; 'copper ladies' broke up the rocks with heavy hammers, while children carried the ore to the kilns, where it was roasted to extract the copper. Meanwhile, the air filled with thick fumes.

Copper from these mines was exported all over the world, and, as Ptolemy remarks, the little port of Amlwch must have been extremely busy. Perhaps one of Williams's most surprising customers was the British navy, which was using copper to clad the bottoms of ships. Copper cladding had the important effect of protecting the timbers from a wood-eating sea worm that could destroy ocean-going craft. In 1784 Williams obtained a new patent, which allowed him to supply sheathing and copper bolts for the navy's ships. Naval commanders, meanwhile, were finding that copper-bottomed ships had another advantage: weed and barnacles did not grow on the copper, so the ships slipped easily through the water. Some said that the extra speed gave British ships the edge at decisive battles such as Trafalgar.

Production peaked between 1788 and 1792, by which time there were some thirty-one smelting furnaces dotted around Amlwch port. But after this period other British mines started to compete with Williams. In addition, the quality and quantity of the ore coming out of the mountain's great opencast mines was falling, and production was steadily declining by the time Williams died in 1802.

The remaining good ore lay much deeper underground, so a new mine manager, James Treweek, was brought in from Cornwall. Treweek introduced deep-shaft mining techniques like those used in his home county. Soon, production was up again, and a windmill and later a beam engine were used to pump water out of the shaft. This gave the mine a new life, and miners were kept busy until underground working stopped in 1883. But there was still copper in the water that came off the mountain, and this could be extracted using the precipitation process. The process continued until the 1930s, when the great precipitation pits were finally abandoned and 4,000 years of copper extraction in this part of Wales finally came to an end.

There is huge potential at Amlwch and Parys to restore some of the remaining buildings and to link the two places with a heritage trail. To do so would not only give an important resource to this corner of Wales, but it would also make people aware of a whole industry and way of life that have been forgotten for too long.

BELOW LEFT *The nineteenth-century engine house still stands – minus its roof – amid the rugged landscape of Parys.*

BELOW RIGHT *A close-up of the windmill's structure reveals rough stone masonry with brick arches above windows and doors.*

Llanelly House LLANELLI

A town house of quality

ABOVE LEFT *Originally Llanelly House had its own gardens to the side and rear. It was not hemmed in by other buildings as it is today.*

ABOVE RIGHT *The staircase is a Victorian addition, lacking the grandeur of the original. But the high windows and classic arch give a hint of the sort of imposing impression this space would have created in Georgian times.*

OPPOSITE *Shutters, panels, cupboards, window surrounds and a host of other details give Llanelli's rooms a rare sense of decorative unity.*

Sometimes it is easy to ignore what is under your nose. Llanelly House is right in the centre of the south Welsh town of Llanelli. Its rows of sash windows mark it out as a major eighteenth-century building, but part of its ground façade is hidden by shop-fronts and a busy road passes right past its main front, making the building difficult even to look at. The house is a forgotten architectural gem.

In the early eighteenth century, Llanelli was a small town. The Industrial Revolution, which was to turn the place into a centre for mining and steel-making, was far in the future. When local woman Margaret Vaughan inherited a house in the middle of the quiet and pleasant town in 1705, it was natural that she should want to live here. A few years later she married Sir John Stepney, a well-connected man from Pembrokeshire, who was close to the court in London. Soon, they were rebuilding Llanelly, and the date 1714 on the rainwater heads suggests that the house was completed by this date. It was one of the finest town houses in Wales.

Llanelly House remained in the Stepney family for much of its lifetime. One influential Stepney, Sir Thomas, inherited the house in 1748. He developed coal mining under his lands, built a lead-smelting works at Pencoed, and owned coal-carrying ships. Thanks to Sir Thomas and his peers, south Wales was industrializing rapidly at this time. Towns became less attractive as homes for the rich, and like many landowning families the Stepneys moved away from their

town house to live in the country. During the years 1772 to 1827, Llanelly was unoccupied by the Stepneys and they even put it on the market several times.

Let to tenants, turned partly into shops and other businesses, used partly as the Stepney estate offices, Llanelly survived into the twentieth century (the Stepneys finally sold the property – to the local authority – in the 1960s). The house suffered numerous alterations – shop-fronts were added, the grand staircase was removed and replaced, eighteenth-century details disappeared behind modern fittings – but many of the architectural details have survived, often hidden by panels of plywood, waiting to be rediscovered and restored.

The outside of the house preserves a number of eighteenth-century details, which are best appreciated by standing back and looking at the building from the churchyard across the road. As in many towns, church and big house are close neighbours, and at Llanelli the churchyard faces the front of the house. From here, the rows of elegant sash windows, the straight parapet hiding the roof, the rendered walls and the panelled doors are all typical eighteenth-century features. Extra decoration, such as the pilasters – flattened decorative columns that rise up the building – and the row of urns along the parapet, mark this out as a high-status building. There are also hints of lost details, such as the bases of balconies that jut out below the upper windows. Without the later shop windows, it would be an elegant, imposing façade.

Light from a distant window leads the eye through a simple but elegant vista along this corridor in Llanelly House.

Inside the house, it seems as if the early architecture has been obliterated by modern alterations. But a closer look reveals that many interior 'walls' are in fact chipboard or plywood panels that have been installed over the original eighteenth-century decorations. As Marianne observes, these modern additions have actually protected the original decorative scheme. Remove the panels and many old details reappear. Tall skirting boards cover the bases of the walls. Moulded dado rails run around the rooms at waist height, to protect the walls from being scratched or knocked by the backs of chairs. Plaster cornices adorn the junctions of walls and ceilings. Between these details, the walls are panelled in wood, each panel surrounded by mouldings in typical eighteenth-century style. A host of other details, from pilasters to fine fireplaces, adds to the impression. It is a style of decoration that evokes an age of elegance.

ABOVE LEFT *A detail of a fire surround gives an impression of the high quality of the decorations in the house.*

ABOVE RIGHT *Looking across the nearby churchyard, one can appreciate the elegance of the front and the hint of ostentation provided by the row of urns along the skyline.*

All this is impressive enough, but there is more. Over some of the fireplaces the panels are painted with landscape and seascape scenes in oils. Such lavish decoration was only available to the richest patrons. The scenes are dark and discoloured by years of dirt and cigar smoke, but they are still precious and rare.

Remove the plywood, clean and redecorate the walls, and many of Llanelly's rooms would be close to their original glory. Some of the second-floor rooms, indeed, have never been hidden behind modern fittings. According to Ptolemy, these are rooms that in most eighteenth-century houses would have been used by servants. They would have been left bare, with plain walls and few decorative details. But at Llanelly, the second-floor rooms are panelled. Some of their elegant fireplaces even have painted landscapes, like those on the lower floors. Rooms like this tell us that Llanelly was always a very important house indeed.

This quality is felt again on the staircase. Here, time has a sadder tale to tell. The original staircase has been removed, and today a Victorian replacement stands in its place. The stair itself – both treads and banisters – are more cramped than those that the first Stepneys would have known. But the actual hall in which the staircase stands is magnificent. A tall space, rising the full three-storey height of the house, takes the breath away. An elaborately moulded classical side entrance leads into the space. This tall, light room would have made a worthy heart to the original house.

Llanelly is in many ways a textbook example of early eighteenth-century architecture. But its painted panels and grand scale make it exceptional in Wales, where grand houses of this period are rare. It could also be a special building for Llanelli. The damage caused by subsidence, damp and modern development needs to be addressed. Restored and shielded from the traffic by pedestrianization, it could provide a cultural centre and museum, with its own restaurant and space for courses and other events. The restored building would become a much-needed heart for Llanelli and a centrepiece for the town's regeneration. And people would start to admire the building once more.

HIGHLAND SCOTLAND

RESTORATION

Kinloch Castle ISLE OF RUM

Easthouse Croft WEST BURRA

Glen o' Dee Sanatorium BANCHORY

Scotland forms a large and important part of the United Kingdom, long separate from England and still fiercely independent and rightly proud of its continuing traditions of culture, science, education and the law. But Scotland often gets short shrift in books about the British regions – perhaps because it is in many places thinly populated, perhaps because much of it is remote from the influential south of England. This book, taking its cue from the television series it accompanies, attempts to avoid this bias by including two chapters on Scotland, one on the Highlands and islands, another on the Lowlands.

The Highlands stretch from Loch Lomond and the Firth of Tay north to John o' Groats. A land of mountains, lochs and glens, this is what outsiders think of when they think of Scotland. An overwhelmingly rural area in which the majority of people live in small communities and on isolated farms, the Highlands have a stunning landscape with a troubled history. If they feel isolated, Scotland's groups of islands, from the Hebrides to Orkney and Shetland, are even lonelier.

Scotland's earliest past can be glimpsed in just these isolated spots. On the Western Isles are standing stones that date back thousands of years, hinting at ancient ritual and religion. Still more evocative are the ancient stone houses of Skara Brae on Orkney. Not far from the coast, these prehistoric dwellings had been covered in sand for perhaps 4,500 years before they were revealed by a storm in 1850. Built of local stones, their walls were protected by earth banks and turf roofs. Light came in only through the small doors, so the dwellings must have been dark inside. But there was a central hearth, providing flickering firelight to illuminate the stone box beds on which the occupants lay and the stone shelves on which they kept their belongings. Nearly everything had to be made of stone here, because there were virtually no trees on the island. As a result, these unique fixtures and fittings have survived the millennia.

The Scottish people of the Iron Age were also notable builders in stone. In around 700 BC they began to defend themselves by building towers called brochs. These towers are found only in Scotland. Occurring mainly in the north and west, they are round, with double dry-stone walls. In the centre of the structure is a courtyard, which acted as a place of refuge for people and livestock in times of insecurity or war. The broch on the island of Mousa, in Shetland, is one of the best preserved. It is about forty-two feet high, and a staircase rises through the gap between the twin walls, leading originally to a rampart that gave a view over the island.

The traditional highland house had a simple, two-room plan with a central door. Here, there is also the original porch, which keeps the wind out of the rooms and shelters anyone arriving at the front door, and the house has had extra rooms added in the roof.

In the following centuries, Scotland's people developed forms of rural architecture that changed little for hundreds of years. The traditional smaller house was compact and austere. Many survive, usually isolated or in small groups rather than in villages. Long and low, the earliest houses had a central entrance with two main areas, one for humans, one for livestock. The simplest form of this early house was the blackhouse, a building type developed mainly in the Hebrides and north-west Highlands, which had thick stone walls with few, if any, windows, giving the building a dark interior – hence its name. The walls were topped by a thatched roof supported on a wooden framework. Ropes, weighted down with rocks, were laid over the roof to keep the thatch in place – an important safeguard in the windy Highlands and islands.

Later, the inhabitants often expanded this simple type of house by putting in an attic floor with dormer windows. Alternatively, they could build a new house with separate accommodation alongside for animals and with more conveniences such as chimneys and windows, but still retaining the simple rectangular plan. The usual building material is stone, although this is often covered with render, the local term for which is harling. In some areas, walls were built of mud, which would be plastered to keep out the damp.

A variety of roofing materials can be seen in rural Scotland. In years gone by, thatch was the norm and this can still be seen, especially in isolated rural areas. It can take several forms: the materials include straw, reed, broom, heather and turf. In some places the loose roofing material is still held on with ropes and stones. Today, many thatched roofs have been replaced by slate or pantiles.

Along the coasts, the villages have their own character, as can be seen in fishing communities all over the British Isles. Rendered and white-painted houses, with details such as the large corner stones and window surrounds left plain, cluster together in small groups. Their gables and chimneys often point towards the coast, so that they present mainly blank walls to the cold sea breezes, the windows are on the more sheltered, inland-looking walls.

In the Highlands and islands, many of the country dwellings were abandoned in the eighteenth century and became ruins. This was the result of the breakdown of the clan system, under which tenants had paid rent to their chiefs by performing military service. In the eighteenth century, landlords began to demand payment in money. Most tenants could not afford the rents and their land was bought up by farmers from the Lowlands and England. In the ensuing 'Clearances', huge numbers were evicted from the land their families had farmed for generations. Homeless and poverty-stricken, many were forced to emigrate. In some parts of the Highlands, their ruined crofts stand as a sad feature of the landscape.

More spectacular remains survive from Scotland's medieval past. There are tower houses in the Highlands, just as there are in Lowland Scotland. In the Highlands, there are some excellent examples of their elaboration, since both kings and great lairds developed their tower houses into full-blown castles. In buildings such as Glamis Castle, near Forfar, and Crathes Castle, south-west of Aberdeen, the tower-house ancestry is still clear to see, for these are tall structures with round corner turrets. At Crathes, for example, the builders seem to have wanted to create a truly striking outline. Conical turret roofs, finials, chimneys and stepped gables point towards the sky. There are battlements, too, but as this castle grew over the years they got smaller and became less functional, while still adding to the overall effect of the dramatic skyline. Such castles seem to be the epitome of medieval Scotland. They also have an affinity with some of the French castles of the Loire Valley, reminding us that the links between Scotland and France go back centuries to the time when the two nations were united against the English.

The castle at Scalloway, Shetland, is a tower house built on an L-shaped plan in the early 1600s.

The dramatic curve of the Glenfinnan railway viaduct makes it one of the most memorable structures in the Highlands. The viaduct carries the West Highland Railway through beautiful countryside near Loch Shiel.

Some of the attributes of the tower house were imitated by later architects to create the baronial style, popular in Scottish country houses of the nineteenth century, such as Torosay Castle on the Isle of Mull. The stepped gables, the turrets with conical roofs often corbelled out from the walls, and the general massiveness of the masonry were all features taken from the older fortified houses to create an impression of ancient grandeur. But baronial-style houses are much more consciously 'designed' than their medieval predecessors. Unlike the early tower houses, they may have symmetrical façades or at least a balanced composition of doors, windows and other elements.

But the Highlands are not all towers and turrets. The fashion for the classical style, fostered by the enlightenment leaders in Edinburgh, also spread northwards. Renowned Scottish architect William Adam, for example, built the restrained classical Haddo House in Aberdeenshire in the 1730s for the Second Earl of Aberdeen. Stone-built, sash-windowed and with twin curving staircases up to the main doorway, it shows how the Highlands could accommodate a mix of English and Italian classical styles.

Scotland's industrial boom of the eighteenth and nineteenth centuries was to begin with confined to the central Lowlands and had its most dramatic impact in the cities. But the rural Highlands had their industry, too. Many workshops wove cloth produced from the wool of Scotland's sheep, and in some places the industry took on a larger scale. The Highlands and islands have plenty of surviving mills, testimony to the textile industry that has long been a source of income in Scotland. Some are still working, their busy machinery on show to visitors. A notable one, Islay Woollen Mill on the island of the same name, has a remarkable array of early machinery that is still functioning. Another notable local industrial building type is the whisky distillery, some of which have traditional kilns with pointed, pagoda-like roofs.

These old local industries carried on through centuries, while industrial upheavals were happening elsewhere. But by the end of the eighteenth century there was a sense that the Highlands would for ever lag behind the rich cities of the south unless communications were improved. This was, after all, an area of mountains and tracks, isolated communities and unoccupied wastes. The sea provided one of the best transport routes and in the early nineteenth century Sir John Sinclair set about improving one harbour, at Wick, in the far north east. Sinclair brought in renowned engineer Thomas Telford, and the men soon built a modern village and installed up-to-date harbour facilities. The herring industry expanded and other businesses sprang up near the harbour.

This was only one aspect of Telford's work in Scotland. He was also involved in a canal project that aimed to link Inverness in the east with Fort William on the west coast along the Great Glen, to provide a route across the entire Highland region. The glen is flooded in many places by lochs including Oich, Ness and Dochfour, so Telford's task was to create a series of links that became known as the Caledonian Canal. Some of Telford's structures on the canal can still be seen. Neptune's Staircase, for example, is a flight of eight locks at Banavie near Fort William. They were state-of-the-art engineering at the time and are still impressive today.

It was towards the end of the nineteenth century that communications in the Highlands were further improved with the arrival of the railways. In 1894 the West Highland Railway pushed northwards from Glasgow to reach Fort William. The engineers then extended it further towards Mallaig on the coast, where it connected with the ferry to Skye. In order to do this, a huge, snaking viaduct had to be built. This is one of Britain's most dramatic railway structures, 380 metres long and thirty metres high in the middle of its sweeping curve. Amazingly, it is built of concrete – once more, the remote Highlands were exploiting cutting-edge technology.

Kinloch Castle ISLE OF RUM

Belgravia in the Western Isles

ABOVE LEFT *An early twentieth-century photograph shows the massive masonry of Kinloch Castle looking almost as good as new.*

ABOVE RIGHT *Even fittings such as the downpipe brackets are beautifully detailed.*

OPPOSITE *The castle's reception rooms still preserve a sense of Victorian richness.*

Kinloch Castle is remote and little known. It stands, foursquare and brown against a background of heather, on the island of Rum in the Inner Hebrides. It looks imposing from the outside – a mass of masonry, battlements and turrets that could only be Scottish. Yet its secrets are inside, and they are unique.

Kinloch Castle was built in the 1850s for William Bullough, one of the richest men in Britain. Bullough was from a Lancashire manufacturing family who made their money in the mills of the Industrial Revolution. The founder of the family fortune was James Bullough, who was born in around 1800 and came up with a string of inventions that streamlined the weaving industry. He and his son grew rich on these inventions, making products, such as a patent spindle, that were bought by every cloth manufacturer. They were soon fabulously rich.

George Bullough, James's grandson, was more interested in the high life than in the family business. He bought a vast 220-foot steam yacht and decided to build himself an equally enormous holiday home on the island of Rum, which was already owned by his family. The result, in Marianne's words, was the 'pure ostentation' of Kinloch Castle.

From the outside, Kinloch Castle is very much of its time. For some decades, Scottish landowners had been building houses in the baronial style that mimicked the castles of the Middle Ages. Kinloch embodies this style.

The masonry is in huge blocks, carefully carved to look rustic. The skyline is alive with round corner turrets and battlements. A big square tower looks out over the island. But there are also large square and bay windows, and rows of decorative arches on the ground floor. These features would never be seen on a real castle, which was built for defence. They hint that houses like Kinloch were designed for comfort and convenience as well as for their impressive appearance.

How comfortable and convenient can be seen inside, where an extraordinary collection of fixtures and fittings survives, many as they were used by the family over eighty years ago. They make Kinloch a true time capsule of Edwardian life. Entering the house, the first thing that strikes us is that many of the actual furnishings are still present. From chairs and sofas to bearskin rugs and drapes, they are all here. The billiard table still waits for a group of well-fed Edwardian gentlemen to assemble around it and pick up their cues. The drawing room seems to wait for afternoon tea or an after-dinner gathering. Wood-panelled corridors look as they did when whole parties of guests were shown to their rooms. As Ptolemy says, it is almost as if these people left yesterday.

A close-up of the veranda arches shows how their smooth masonry contrasts with the rustic effect of the main castle walls.

ABOVE LEFT *This shallow sink is something of a mystery. Since the nearby windows are fitted with shutters to keep out the light, it may have originally been used for processing photographic plates.*

ABOVE RIGHT *A library of volumes waits for readers to return.*

Look a little closer and the house is a real museum of Victorian features. Light fittings, from glowing glass bowls to glittering chandeliers, are all preserved. And for a house this old and this remote they are special, for Kinloch had its own hydroelectric plant, lighting the whole house with electricity. Another advanced feature of life at Kinloch was the telephone: the house had its own internal telephone exchange, a first for Scotland.

Bullough's bathroom is beautifully appointed, with a bath big enough to wallow in. The taps are also enormous, but they are not amazing for their size but because of what they do. They control a shower system that is as sophisticated as a modern power shower, with a range of different settings that make water pour down from above or jet out from the sides. For a time when most people had to bathe in a tin container in front of the kitchen fire, it is astounding.

The Victorians loved technology, and the bathroom is just one example that does its job efficiently and without fuss. A more showy example is the orchestrion, a Victorian device for playing music that was designed to summon up the sound of an entire orchestra. The music was encoded in a series of holes on a roll of paper. The machine 'read' the holes, rather as the laser in a CD player reads tiny pits in a CD, and activated all sorts of instruments, from shiny brass trumpets to a big drum. Very few of these large machines were made; this one is said to have been ordered originally by the royal family for their house at Balmoral. It seems at home among the gadgets at Kinloch.

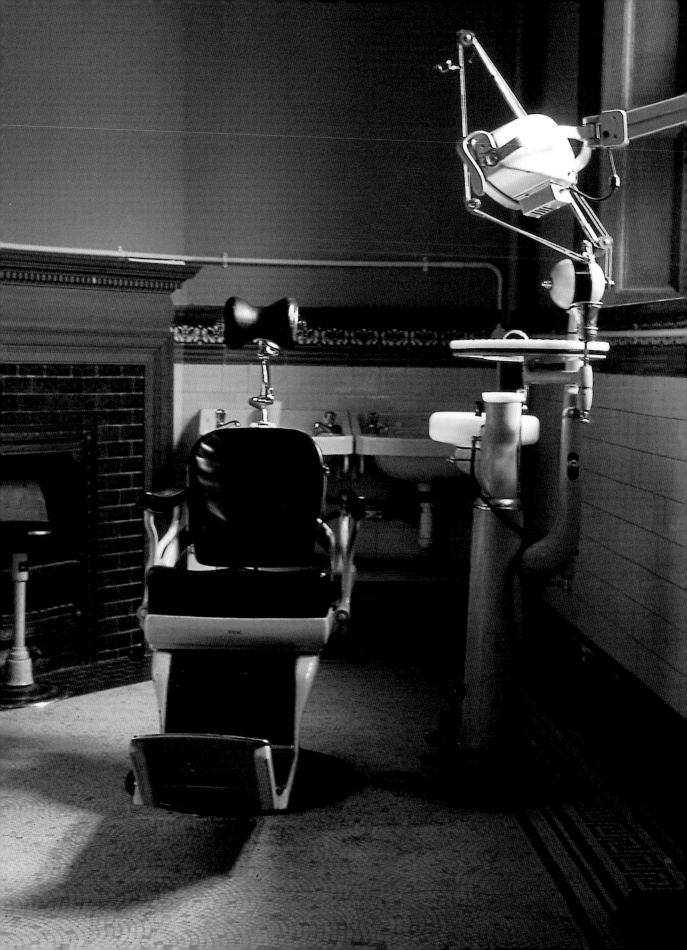

ABOVE LEFT *The mechanism of the orchestrion still displays a glistening array of pipes, drums and other instruments.*

ABOVE RIGHT *Stained-glass panels throw a warm light into the corner of a room.*

OPPOSITE *In the 1950s a dental surgery was set up in one room in the castle. Local people could come here for treatment, to save a trip to the mainland.*

Decoratively, the house is outstanding, too. Wooden panelling, made to the highest specification, is everywhere. The main rooms have ornate plaster ceilings, while the walls are covered with the original nineteenth-century silk. Many windows have panels of stained glass in floral designs with a Victorian feel that also looks forward to the curvaceous Art Nouveau style of the end of the century.

The house was a fitting setting for a life of luxury. For just eight weeks a year the Bulloughs came here and threw lavish parties. High society came here in droves; there was shooting in the daytime, dining in the evening. All this went on until the First World War, when forty of the servants went to fight in the trenches; only two returned at the end of the war. And by this time social life had changed. The Bulloughs came here less often, the extravagant way of life faded away and eventually the family gave up their island holiday home. For a while Kinloch was a hotel, but then it remained empty, slowly decaying while the island around it became a nature reserve.

This time warp of a house looks remarkably well preserved. But it is seriously threatened. Water is penetrating the structure, as is clear from peeling plasterwork and stains on the wall coverings. Examining the roof, Ptolemy and Marianne point to splitting lead and gaping joints between stones as the main culprits. Problems like these need to be tackled soon to protect both the house and its unique contents. Then ambitious plans to turn Kinloch into a living museum and hostel for visitors to Rum's nature reserve may come to fruition.

Easthouse Croft WEST BURRA

A unique Shetland survival

Easthouse was built with the most basic materials – rubble masonry, a turf roof, and a simple wooden-framed window.

Shetland is the most northerly part of Britain, a cluster of about a hundred rocky, windswept islands as close to Norway as they are to Aberdeen. For hundreds of years, crofting was the usual way of life on Shetland. There were perhaps 5,000 houses altogether, and most of those outside the two main towns of Lerwick and Scalloway were crofts, groups of farm buildings around a small stone house. Only two remain today. One is a museum, and the other, Easthouse, is empty and in need of restoration, so that future generations can learn about the crofting way of life.

Easthouse is on West Burra, an island to the west of Shetland's mainland. Well away from the islands' main towns, the place seems isolated to outsiders, but it has supported many families in a scattered crofting community for generations. In fact, people have lived on Shetland for over 5,000 years, and even remote West Burra has been inhabited since the seventh century, as shown by the date of carved Christian stones found on the island, proving that this was home to one of Britain's most far-flung religious communities.

We do not know much about the lives of these early inhabitants. But they must have relied on the island's resources as much as the crofters of the nineteenth and twentieth centuries did. In particular, Burra's climate, though northern, is warmed by the Gulf Stream. This makes both East and West Burra well placed to tap into the rich fishing grounds of Burra Haff. No doubt these early people were also using natural local materials to build houses similar to the croft that survives at Easthouse.

Crofters were small tenant farmers, raising sheep, both for their wool and their meat, as well as keeping a few hens and pigs. A crofter used much of his farm's produce to feed himself and his family. The wool was spun and knitted by the women of the house. A further source of income came from fishing, for nowhere on Shetland is far from the sea.

The farmers needed this extra income because they had to pay rent for their crofts. In addition, they had to repair their own houses, and this was the cause of many disputes between tenant and laird at the end of the nineteenth century. Farmer, fisherman and builder – the Shetland crofter had to be a master of all trades.

Like its ruined neighbours, Easthouse is made in the Shetland way from local materials. Its walls are of stone and are three feet thick to keep the house

OPPOSITE *Even with the roof gone, the solid stone walls of the farm buildings survive.*

ABOVE LEFT *Removing the modern plasterboard panels from their supporting wooden framework reveals the walls covered with the original lime plaster.*

ABOVE CENTRE *The layout of the house – one floor, one doorway and a room on either side – is clear from outside.*

ABOVE RIGHT *An early photograph reveals there has been little change to the structure.*

warm in winter and cool in summer. Most of the stone is rubble, but there are large squared stones at the corners to give the structure extra strength. At the wall tops they are covered with a pebbledash render made of beach pebbles and lime mortar. Inside, the walls have been lined with modern plasterboard, but beneath the old finish this can be seen. This was made up of a layer of lime plaster, laid quite roughly and bound by animal hair incorporated into the mixture, and a simple covering of coats of limewash. As Ptolemy comments, everything about this use of local material is rooted in common sense.

There are few trees on Shetland, so many of the roof timbers are driftwood. They support a roof covering of typical Shetland thatch made of a layer of turf cut into pieces like tiles and laid, grass-side down, on to the timbers. On top of this was a thatch of straw, which had to be replaced every few years. This was the most regular maintenance required by these sturdy houses.

The plan of the house is very simple – there is only the ground floor and it is divided into just two rooms. One would have been for living and cooking; a thick wooden beam across one wall suggests that this was the site of the original fireplace. The other room was a bedroom. The accommodation seems cramped by modern standards, and few Shetlanders today would give up their modern bungalows for the chance to live in an old croft house. But in former times there was little privacy and no luxury. People made do with the space they had and anyway spent much of their lives outdoors.

At the back of the house is a compact yard that was the focus of much of this life. A barn, byre, pigsty and henhouse are all stone walled and preserve remains of their thatched roofs. All these small outbuildings are close to the house and easy to reach from the back door. Around the complex is a landscape dotted with the ruins of similar crofts, many close to modern bungalows.

Buildings like this have been central to the life of Shetland for years. No one knows exactly when most of them were built, because written records before the late nineteenth century are thin on the ground. But there was certainly a

croft here in 1832, when a rental survey of Burra was made. The sketch map that accompanied the survey positioned a croft house on the site of the current building. Another record comes from 1890, when Sinclair Eunson gave evidence at a Crofters' Commission hearing. Eunson said that he had occupied his croft for sixty years, so it may have been newly built at the time of the 1832 survey. The last permanent tenant of Easthouse was Jim Anderson, Sinclair's great-great-grandson. He maintained and cared for the house but moved out when his family outgrew it in 1972.

After the Andersons left the croft it was used for a while by construction workers who were building an oil terminal. Then it did duty as a holiday cottage during the tourist season. But since the late 1980s it has been empty. Recently, local people have been trying to raise money to restore the croft for use by community and educational groups as a heritage centre and for small meetings and exhibitions. Like Ptolemy and Marianne, they know that hundreds of grand country houses have been preserved while only two crofts remain. They are aware that if Easthouse is allowed to decay, evidence of this special way of life will vanish for ever. Easthouse provides one last chance to save a building of this type.

A more distant view shows some of the farm buildings that adjoin the house.

Glen o' Dee Sanatorium BANCHORY

In splendid isolation

ABOVE LEFT *Armorial stained glass gives an up-market impression appropriate to attract the well-to-do fee-paying patients of the Glen o' Dee Hospital.*

ABOVE RIGHT *In spite of years of neglect, the hospital's wooden structure has survived very well.*

OPPOSITE *Long corridors run the length of the hospital and sunlight from the patients' rooms floods into these passages.*

Although it looks more like an overgrown Swiss chalet than a Scottish building, the Glen o' Dee Hospital at Banchory is oddly at home in Aberdeenshire, its wooden walls framed by pine trees and its rows of windows giving generous views of the landscape. It is an extraordinary building with an extraordinary story.

Tuberculosis, an infection of the lungs, was one of the major causes of death before the introduction of antibiotic drugs in the 1940s. By the end of the nineteenth century the disease had killed millions in Britain. The only treatment was rest, and patients had to be isolated to prevent the disease from spreading.

In nineteenth-century Germany a new variation on the standard treatment was developed. One of the most important pioneers was Otto Walther, who worked at the sanatorium at Nordrach, near Baden. Walther's treatment involved bed rest until the fever went down; he then gave his patients plenty of fresh air, a nourishing diet and gentle exercise. Walther believed that mountain air was especially beneficial. Another German doctor, Peter Dettweiler, had a theory that the aroma of pine trees was also beneficial to tuberculosis patients. As time went by, sanatoria sprang up everywhere among the mountains and upland pine forests of northern Europe.

Soon, Scotland was following suit. Dr David Lawson of Banchory was a disciple of Walther and a believer in the curative qualities of sunshine and

ABOVE LEFT *A corner of a bathroom reminds the visitor that hygiene, and hot and cold running water, were important considerations for Lawson and his patients.*

ABOVE RIGHT *Elegant glazed doors and screens divide the public rooms, allowing natural light to penetrate from one area to another.*

fresh air. At the very end of the nineteenth century he planned his own sanatorium along German lines. He realized that Scotland was an ideal location because of the high levels of winter sunshine and low rainfall, and he saw that he could maximize these benefits by designing rooms with large, south-facing windows. By building the hospital next to pine woods he could even expose his patients to the scent of the needles that Dr Dettweiler thought was so beneficial.

The Banchory sanatorium was built mainly of wood, an inexpensive material, and the carpenters could erect the walls of the large building quickly. Wood is a low-technology material, as Ptolemy insists. But although cheap, the pine used was of good quality – a strong, resinous wood that has kept out the water until fairly recently. Well built and insulated with a matting material made of sheep's wool, it provided a warm, comfortable environment. It also allowed an attractive design, the chalet-like appearance suggesting a similar approach to Alpine hospitals in Europe. The rows of windows and balconies are welcoming and look good as well as providing the kind of accommodation Lawson required. The long wings of pine are arranged on either side of the single stone feature, an imposing, tall tower containing the hospital's water tank; the tower was built of granite to support the weight of the tank.

A lot of thought went into the design of the hospital. The building is long and slender, so that all the patients' rooms can face south. Each of these rooms has large windows to let in plenty of sunlight, and the windowsills are low, so that a bedridden patient could both admire the view and benefit from the rays of the sun. Each room opens on to a balcony, so that patients could get fresh air without having to take a long walk. Originally, there were also wooden shutters that let a controlled amount of outside air into the rooms, so that the patients could even breathe fresh air when they were asleep. This complete

adoption of Walther's ideas about fresh air and sunlight in the treatment of tuberculosis earned the hospital the nickname of 'Nordrach-on-Dee'.

Many small details in the design, from the stained-glass panels in some of the windows, kept small so that they do not block out too much sunlight, to the detailing of the outside woodwork, suggest that Lawson wanted the building to be pleasant and attractive. After all, this was a private sanatorium, where patients had to pay to be admitted. For some, it was an alternative to a long trip to a hospital in Germany or Switzerland. The patients would have expected a high standard of care, comfort and decoration for their money.

Lawson emphasized the comforts offered to patients. He stressed the heating by 'steam pipes', the supply of hot and cold water available to patients and the electric lighting. He also provided a well-appointed dining room and a small library. Furnishings were more luxurious than in most hospitals, and public rooms, from the entrance foyer to the dining room, were well designed, incorporating features such as coved ceilings and stained glass. The building was also technically advanced, with a full range of laboratory facilities, its own X-ray department and various specialized treatment rooms.

The sanatorium at Banchory treated tuberculosis sufferers from its opening in 1900 until it closed in 1928. A few years later, like many former sanatoria, it started a new life as a hotel. Its south-facing rooms, well-appointed public spaces and beautiful setting made it ideal for this function. The long interconnected verandas were turned into private balconies, one for each room, an electric lift was put in, a new drive constructed and many of the old nurses' rooms made over for the use of guests' maids and chauffeurs. The hospital's public spaces were also redecorated to provide lounges and smoking rooms. Then, after a spell housing troops during the Second World War, the Scottish Red Cross Society bought the building and ran it as a hospital for ex-servicemen and women. Later, it was transferred to the National Health Service and was vacated when more modern hospital buildings were developed nearby. It now stands empty.

It may be that when Lawson built his wooden sanatorium, he expected it to have quite a short life. If there had ever been a problem with the spread of infection, it would not have been difficult to burn down the whole structure – with the exception of the great granite water tower. But the building has lasted very well. Although the paint is peeling and the structure is now letting in the rain, it could be rescued. Its south-facing rooms let in as much sunlight as they ever did, and, as Marianne is quick to notice, its wooden façade and gables still work well in the landscape. Plans for the future involve the provision of care accommodation for the elderly upstairs, with public rooms, display spaces and a café below. Young and old alike could enjoy this beautiful building once more.

LOWLAND SCOTLAND

KEEP OUT
DANGEROUS
BUILDING

RESTORATION

'Britannia Music Hall is an extraordinary surviving example of a building that was for the people. It's particularly important to try and preserve some of our popular culture.'

Steve Punt champions
BRITANNIA MUSIC HALL

'This linoleum factory is part of a fine industrial heritage that enabled Britain to be great. We should commemorate those achievements and the suffering of the people who worked in harsh conditions during the Industrial Revolution.'

Michael Portillo champions
NAIRN'S LINO FACTORY

'Mavisbank says so much about Scotland at the beginning of the eighteenth century, when it was regarded as an extraordinary, modern building. It's an incredibly important part of not just Scotland's heritage, but the rest of Britain's as well.'

Kirsty Wark champions
MAVISBANK

The area known as the Scottish Lowlands stretches from the English border to Loch Lomond and the Firth of Tay. Although the area contains hills, such as the Southern Uplands, it is generally lower-lying than northern Scotland. From Roman times to the late Middle Ages, the area's history was dominated by disputes with the area south of the border. As a result, the Scots found that it paid to be well defended and local families in the medieval period developed the tower house to protect their people and goods. Tower houses are tall structures with strong, thick walls. They usually have a small doorway with a door that can be secured with a drawbar. Above are small, barred windows and at the top is a parapet, which can overhang the walls and has crenellations to protect defending men-at-arms. A typical interior contains a stone-vaulted basement storage area, a first-floor main hall, and private chambers above.

Early tower houses are square in plan but in later buildings extra wings and corner turrets were added. Tower houses were built until the seventeenth century, but by this time convenience was often a higher priority than defence, so their strength became more symbolic – their windows tended to be larger and their rooms more comfortable. Later still, they became broader, rectangular houses, with more chambers to satisfy the growing desire for privacy. But in many places, the smaller, more austere medieval towers remain, a very Scottish contribution to the history of architecture. There are examples all over Scotland, one of the best is Craigmillar Castle, south-east of Edinburgh.

Such tower houses are usually found in rural areas but many of Scotland's most notable lowland buildings are in the country's towns and cities. The major centres, Edinburgh and Glasgow, are famous, attracting visitors from all over the world. People come for the unique atmosphere, for the prestigious cultural events and for the history. All Scotland's major cities date back at least to the Middle Ages, when they were centres of religion and education. But, just like the cities of the south, they expanded beyond recognition. The Industrial Revolution played a large part in this growth, as did the huge trading opportunities that opened up as Britain's empire grew during the nineteenth century. In spite of this, earlier buildings do survive in Edinburgh and Glasgow, but the overwhelming impression of these cities comes from the industrial age.

Edinburgh's Palace of Holyroodhouse combines castle-like turrets with classical Renaissaince details – a very Scottish blend of styles.

To sample the atmosphere of an early Scottish town, therefore, you have to visit a smaller place, such as Culross, an old fishing and trading port on the Firth of Forth. Culross began as a religious centre – the remains of a medieval abbey can be seen – but in the Middle Ages it became a centre of a thriving coal and salt trade with northern Europe. The local mines and the port grew, and merchants and mine owners built themselves solid pale-rendered red-tiled houses in and around the marketplace.

Many of these survive, some with striking stepped gables, to give much of Culross the atmosphere of a sixteenth-century Scottish town. With their pine-panelled interior walls and painted ceilings, the houses are warm and welcoming. Their owners were obviously rich, but were not ostentatious. The largest of these houses, the outstanding ochre-coloured Palace, was built for the richest of them all, the sixteenth-century mine owner, Sir George Bruce.

Like Culross, many of Scotland's major cities are in the central Lowlands, near the Firths of Forth and Clyde, the two great waterways that provided access to wealth through fishing, trade and shipbuilding. The area that is now Edinburgh was occupied in prehistoric times, and Bronze Age settlers built fortifications on a high rocky outcrop that was one of the easiest places in the area to defend. In the Middle Ages this became Castle Rock, the site of a royal fortress, and Edinburgh itself grew around the castle's walls. The city thrived in the late Middle Ages as the capital of independent Scotland but declined again in the seventeenth century, a time of bitter religious disputes between Catholics and Protestants. In the eighteenth century, however, the city's fortunes took a turn for the better. The Act of Union in 1707 ensured that Scotland could keep its religious independence and legal system, and the stage was set for Edinburgh to blossom as an intellectual and cultural centre. It still plays this role today.

Edinburgh Castle is a reminder of the city's medieval might. The castle's tiny Romanesque chapel is said to have been built after the death of St Margaret, wife of King Malcolm III, in 1093. The fifteenth-century royal apartments are also preserved, but in addition the castle contains remains from later periods, such as fortifications dating from the seventeenth century and the eighteenth-century governor's house. The whole forms a huge complex that evokes much of Edinburgh's history.

From the castle, a series of ancient streets known collectively as the Royal Mile passes through the middle of the Old Town. Its buildings include seventeenth-century merchants' houses and tall old tenement blocks, the ancestors of the apartment buildings still lived in by many urban Scots. Nearby are narrow alleys and closes that recall the plan of the medieval city.

The High Kirk of Edinburgh, also known as St Giles' Cathedral, dominates the Royal Mile. Its Gothic tower is its most striking feature, its ornate carved top earning it the nickname of 'the crown of St Giles'. The great church is also ornate inside, especially in the Thistle Chapel, which is a marvel of intricate sculpture and vaulting in honour of the Order of the Thistle. With its painted coats of arms, it seems to sum up the age of chivalry.

At the opposite end of the Royal Mile from the castle stands the Palace of Holyroodhouse, a royal residence dating from the sixteenth century. Its façades are full of rectangular windows and classical details in the Scottish Renaissance style, which is also seen in other grand Scottish buildings of this date, such as Falkland Palace and Crichton Castle. Scotland had close links with Continental Europe at this time, and the style is influenced by the trailblazing architecture of Italy and France.

In the eighteenth century Edinburgh expanded radically. The streets of the Old Town had become cramped and insanitary, and in 1752 the Lord Provost launched a scheme for the building of a New Town to the north of the castle. A competition to design the development was launched, and in 1767 the young architect James Craig was announced as the winner. His elegant layout of terraces, squares and gently curving crescents, all built in stone, was an object lesson in town planning. The authorities introduced a set of rules to regulate the builders – standard-width pavements, aligned façades, fixed numbers of storeys and a ban on dormer windows – which, together with a consistent use of sash windows, panelled doors and classical details, give the buildings of the New Town a unity that was unknown in Edinburgh before this time. The spacious houses and apartments are sought after to this day.

The New Town is the most remarkable area of Edinburgh, a reminder of the time when the city was a Mecca for philosophers and inventors, earning it the nickname 'Athens of the north'. Edinburgh has later architectural monuments,

Rusticated masonry and panelled doors topped with fanlights are two of the hallmarks of the houses in Edinburgh's New Town.

*The Glasgow tenements have large
windows arranged in angle bays so
that the rooms catch the sun at
different times of the day.*

from the great Victorian hall of the Royal Museum, with its cathedral-like
slender pillars and glass roof, to the new Scottish Parliament Building by the
Catalan architect Enric Miralles. But the city's glory is its eighteenth-century
streets.

The highlight of Glasgow's architecture, on the other hand, is its nineteenth-
and twentieth-century buildings. Glasgow's history goes back much further
than this, of course. It was a centre for religion and learning in the Middle
Ages, and a major port in the eighteenth century. Its main trade was with the
British colonies, especially the tobacco-growing areas in America and the
Caribbean; 'tobacco barons', grown rich from the trade, dominated the life of
the city and took over other trades – in sugar, cotton and tea, for example.
Soon, Glasgow was booming.

There was industry here, too. Mining, cotton weaving and shipbuilding
expanded through the eighteenth century, and people flocked to the city to
work in the mines and mills. They were followed by more and more incomers,
many of them Highlanders who had been forced to leave their lands in the
notorious 'Clearances'. The expansion continued as Glasgow became the
second largest city in Britain's vast world empire.

Evidence of this boom of trade and industry is still thick on the ground.
George Square in the centre of the city began life as a residential
development but by the nineteenth century, with the expansion of trade and
the coming of the railways, many of its buildings became hotels. Later, it
turned into the administrative heart of the city when in 1888 the vast Glasgow
City Chambers was built along one whole side of the square. Outside this
building presents a vast façade of columns and multiple domes to the square.
Its interior contains magnificent, marble-clad staircases, vaulted ceilings
emblazoned with gold leaf, and grand Renaissance-style rooms.

Designs like the City Chambers are hugely confident, speaking of a city that
could take on the world and win. And sometimes it seemed as if Glasgow's
architects could take on any style in the world, too. One of the most
outlandish and outstanding is Templeton's Carpet Factory, to the south-east
of the city centre near Glasgow Green. This is an extravaganza in multi-
coloured brick, tiles and sandstone, built in 1889 in imitation of the Doge's
Palace in Venice. The zigzag patterns traced by the brickwork, as well as
being Venetian in origin, seem to mirror the designs of the carpets made
within, so that the building became a huge advertisement for its products.

Other experiments were inspired by Glasgow's industry, though none were
quite as showy as Templeton's. One that comes near is the six-storey
industrial complex known as the Egyptian Halls in Union Street. Outside, the
building has rows of Egyptian-style columns, tapering towards the top and

crowned with lotus flowers. Inside, everything is much more sober, with rows of cast-iron pillars showing that the architect, Alexander Thompson, was a master of the latest in building technology.

Thirty years later Glasgow's most famous architect of all was also looking towards the future. Charles Rennie Mackintosh designed a series of Glasgow buildings that influenced architects throughout the twentieth century. He blended a range of influences – such as Scottish baronial, European Art Nouveau and Japanese decorative arts – to produce a unique style of his own. Buildings such as Glasgow's School of Art and the Willow Tea Rooms in Sauchiehall Street show this to perfection. Beautifully arranged, asymmetrical façades, big windows and careful use of stained glass and ironwork are all hallmarks of Mackintosh's style. So are his interiors, in which every detail, from light fittings to door knobs, was specially designed. Mackintosh's work is Glasgow's most famous contribution to the story of architecture.

Edinburgh and Glasgow are places of pilgrimage for anyone interested in buildings, but other Scottish cities have much to offer. St Andrews, one of the oldest of them all, is a good place in which to savour Scotland's medieval history. It began as a pilgrimage place, the home of the bones of St Andrew, which were brought here by another saint, Regulus. The cathedral became the largest and most important in Scotland, but it was destroyed during the Reformation of the sixteenth century. Although it remains a ruin, the west front and parts of the apse and south wall still stand to give a hint of what it must have been like. St Andrews was a backwater until the nineteenth century, when a fashion for the game of golf brought visitors to the town. The old university enjoyed a revival in the same period, when new houses joined the city's three ancient main streets, with their stone house fronts and winding back alleys.

Scotland has many other towns and cities, from industrial centres like Arbroath and Dundee to smaller towns such as Perth, which is rich in Georgian buildings, Stirling, with its great castle, and Dumfries, which has houses of pink sandstone. Most have buildings of interest, from churches and town halls to factories and hospitals. Some are obvious monuments; others are hidden gems that the visitor has to seek out. But they all reveal something of Scotland's rich and varied history.

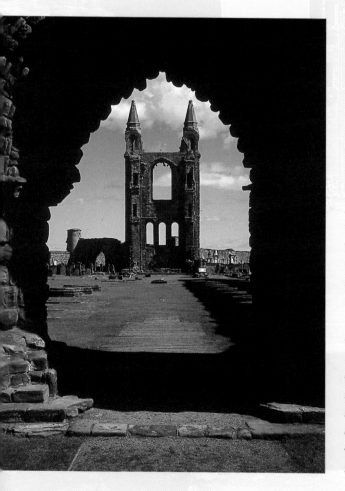

The west front of the ruined cathedral of St Andrews preserves the simple mouldings and pointed window openings of the 1270s.

Britannia Music Hall GLASGOW

From the early stages of music hall

ABOVE LEFT *An early photograph shows the street front of Britannia Music Hall in all its glory. The façade is stepped slightly forward of the surrounding shop fronts, to emphasize its importance.*

ABOVE RIGHT *A close-up of part of the façade shows some of the classical details. The first floor is plastered to give the impression of large blocks of stone with deep joints between them – an effect known as rustication.*

OPPOSITE *Plaster decoration adorns the great sweep of the music hall's coved ceiling.*

High above a modern shop-front on a busy Glasgow street, the flaking front of the old Britannia Music Hall can still be seen. It is an imposing 1830s warehouse, converted in 1857 when the Grecian façade was put on, complete with rows of round-topped windows, a band of Greek key decoration, plaster fruit and a triangular pediment at the top. It looks important – and it was, because this theatre played host to some of the greatest performers of all time. Entertainers such as Dan Leno, Stan Laurel and Jack Buchanan all began their careers here, in front of one of the toughest audiences in the theatrical world.

It all began in 1857, when the music hall was built to provide entertainment for Glasgow's expanding working class. It could hold over a thousand people, and audiences piled in, smoking, drinking and frantic for a good night out. An early notice orders 'no ladies admitted unless accompanied by a gentleman', an indication that prostitution was rife. For the performers there were other problems: members of the audience came equipped with rotten fruit, picked up from the local market, to hurl at the stage if they didn't like what they saw. Worse, there are stories that one of the proprietors handed out steel rivets, which could also be thrown at the stage. The situation was particularly bad, it was said, on amateur night, when anyone with a brave heart and a talent to

amuse could try their luck on stage, dodging projectiles as the crowd grew restive. In the theatrical world it was said that if you could survive the Britannia you could survive anywhere.

Today, the interior seems a sad relic of its former self. In the gloom, you can make out the auditorium surrounded on three sides by balconies with steeply stepped seats. The stage, which is gently raked and quite shallow, is framed by its wooden proscenium and preserves some of the mechanism for suspending scenery. The area is covered with an elaborate plastered coved ceiling.

When the building closed in the late 1930s, an internal floor was put in, cutting the auditorium in two. The upper section stalls did duty as a storeroom and shop. The balcony remained unused except in the Second World War

Upstairs, natural light from the large windows illuminates a scene that has been little disturbed since the building was closed in 1930.

when it was used as a chicken farm. Its brownish paint contrasts with the white and blue 1970s paint that covers much of the lower half. With a bright light and a keen eye, however, it is possible to make out what the Victorian decoration was like. As Marianne observes, where the later paint has peeled or faded, nineteenth-century stencilled roundels and patterns can be seen. This interior was clearly as flamboyant as the artistes who performed on the stage. The surviving hard wooden seats, slender columns and other remains give a fair idea of what the place would have been like.

The Britannia Music Hall must have survived in its original form until the beginning of the twentieth century, when it changed ownership. The new proprietor, A. E. Pickard, transformed the theatre into the early 1900s equivalent of a theme park, which he called Pickard's Panopticon. Sideshows, an exhibition of waxworks and a freak show were the main exhibits. In the basement was a small, cramped zoo, which made the whole place both smelly and at times dangerous. On two occasions a bear escaped, once on to the roof of the building, once into the street, where it terrified passers-by until Pickard shot it. A projection system was also installed, and the Panopticon was one of the first places in the country where people could see the latest form of entertainment – the movies.

The Britannia is special for several reasons. First and foremost, it is one of the most complete early music halls in existence and a very rare survival from the theatrical history of the mid-nineteenth century. Secondly, the music hall has a special place in the history of Victorian Glasgow. The city was full of poor workers, but was also a place of great commercial prosperity,

Ghostly figures look down from the balcony, a haunting reminder of different era of entertainment.

pivotal in the history of the British Empire. In Ptolemy's words, the Britannia offers a unique insight into the life of the city before the arrival of motorways and high-rise blocks. Thirdly, a host of objects, scattered throughout the building, bring it to life in a most unusual way.

Pickard's projection box survives, as do many objects that have been found in the nooks and crannies of the building. Parts of the Britannia, unswept for decades, have yielded the most extraordinary archaeological gold dust. A head from the waxworks, together with bits of games stalls and a coconut shy are evidence of what went on upstairs in the days of Pickard's Panopticon. Smaller items have also been unearthed among the dust: wax fingers from one of the figures displayed by Pickard; buttons, said suggestively by some to be men's fly buttons; gold jewellery, including poignant lost wedding rings; matches and cigarette boxes; confectionery wrappers from small sideshow prizes; riveting nails, which may have been ammunition thrown by discontented spectators.

The Britannia Music Hall, with its flaking paint and plaster, looks fragile, and the building is certainly at risk. But, as Ptolemy says, in many ways it is a very solid building – its walls and roof are still doing the duty they did around 150 years ago. But because the structure is solid, this does not mean that restoration will be straightforward. For example, evidence of the Victorian paint finishes is valuable but fragile. If the removal of modern paint is done carefully, so that conservationists can preserve – or at least record – the old stencil patterns underneath, then the building will have more to tell us about its history and be even more attractive when it is restored. It gives one hope that its seats may be filled once more with a cheering audience – drawn both by a restored music hall and working heritage centre. A renovated Britannia might have a further benefit, bringing visitors and money into the area and helping the wider regeneration of this part of the city.

Nairn's KIRKCALDY

Covering the nation's floors

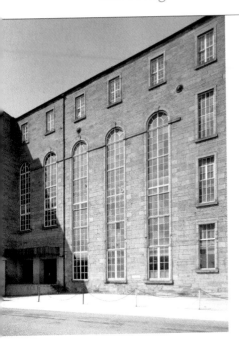

When Nairn's lino factory was in use, the tall, thin windows were the most striking feature of the building.

OPPOSITE *The great windows have survived, their lower sections boarded up to keep out trespassers.*

Lino, or linoleum as it was more properly called, once covered the floors of Britain and much of the world. Cheap, colourful and easy to clean, it was common between the wars and very popular throughout the 1950s and 1960s. Then, thanks to fashions for other floor coverings, from fitted carpet to polished wood, it almost vanished. But for a few decades people took lino for granted. They did not even know where it was made – but the people of Kirkcaldy, Fife, knew very well.

The world's biggest lino producer was Nairn's of Kirkcaldy. They began making lino in 1875, when the patent for the material, invented by Frederick Walton, ran out. Before long, Michael Nairn was putting up an enormous purpose-built lino factory, which he completed in 1882. By this time the people of Kirkcaldy were getting used to the process of lino manufacture. They had to, because it made an awful and pervasive smell. Lino is produced by oxidizing linseed oil to produce a tough, shiny coating that is attached to a flexible backing made of fibres such as jute. The smell of linseed oil, which many compared with rotting fish, became a part of life in Kirkcaldy, instantly recognizable by returning natives as they stepped from the train.

Over the years, a huge complex of over thirteen acres developed around Nairn's original factory. Where there is now open space, there were a dozen factory buildings, a power plant and a clutch of facilities for the employees, including a sports ground and a clinic. The place even had its own fire service. At its height, the company employed more than 8,000 people and sent its linseed-oil smell all over the town. After the decline in the lino market, the site shrank again; most of the buildings were pulled down and production moved elsewhere. The tall 1882 factory building is now all that remains.

James Gillespie was the architect from St Andrews who designed the factory. He drew on the traditional elements of factory design – a tall, rectangular block with rows of windows – but with a difference. On the building's south-facing front, the factory's main windows are enormous, more than forty feet tall. These monumental-looking windows are enhanced by the rugged detailing of the masonry, which is of rough stone with finely dressed blocks for the details. Even today, in its splendid isolation, the factory makes an enormous impact.

The windows were not just put there for show. They light a vast, tall inner

OPPOSITE *At the rear of the building, rows of blocked openings reveal the positions of more large windows. These were bricked up when another structure was built against this wall. The change in colour two-thirds of the way up marks the height of this later structure.*

BELOW LEFT *Concrete uprights support floors that reach right up to the big windows.*

BELOW RIGHT *The factory's masonry, with its massive corner stones, was clearly built to last.*

space, originally forty-seven feet six inches tall from floor to ceiling, where the great ninety-foot lengths of newly printed lino hung to dry. Facing south, the windows helped to speed up the drying process with heat from the sun.

At the back, the north wall is completely different and tells another part of the building's story. The wall is blank now, but it does not take long to make out the filled-in openings of former windows, some blocked with brick, others with stone. Another structure, now demolished, was once built on to this side of the factory, and these marks and blocked openings are the scars it has left behind. They are also fascinating evidence for the historian, tracing the varying fortunes of Nairn's as the buildings expanded and shrank over time.

At first glance the inside of the building is disappointing. When it was first constructed, the building housed two main work spaces: the upper floor, where the lino was printed, and the vast hanging area, where the rolls dried in front of the huge windows. But in the 1930s, as manufacturing methods developed, the use of the building changed. The great inner hall, where the rolls of lino had hung, became a storage area. It was filled with a structure of concrete floors and pillars, each floor between eight and nine feet from its neighbour, so that the standard seven-foot-wide rolls of lino could be accommodated with ease. Meanwhile, the upper floor became a production area, where lino was pieced together by adding 'tiles' of coloured material to rolls of plain jute backing.

During the Second World War the building was used for war work. The largest bombs produced during the war were made here, including those dropped on the raids flown by the famous Dam Busters. Nairn's factory also produced millions of square yards of bituminized felt for repairing roofs damaged in the Blitz, together with some 300 miles of hessian to make beds that were used by Londoners sheltering from air raids.

Further changes of use followed until 1986, when the company was taken over and production was moved to a more modern factory on the other side of the nearby railway line. On this side of the line, everything was demolished except for this single listed building, with its vast windows.

Nairn's lino factory looks in a sorry state today. The floors are a sea of cracking lino fragments. Water and vegetation are getting in. And the 1930s concrete floors obscure the main space, which must once have been breathtaking. But things are not as bad as they seem. Ptolemy notes that the concrete structure has actually helped to preserve the building's strength and stability. And the original shell was so well built that it has not deteriorated as much as many other structures would have done. A number of similar buildings of the late-Victorian period have wooden lintels to support the masonry above the windows; these rot when moisture gets in, putting the stability of the wall at risk. But at Kirkcaldy, the windows are topped by solid arches of stone on the outside and brick within.

Many locals would like to see the factory restored to its former glory. As Ptolemy points out, with a largely sound structure containing plenty of large, flexible spaces, there is every chance of success. A piece of Kirkcaldy's history could be preserved, and there are plenty of potential roles for this type of building. Plans are afoot to create accommodation for new businesses in the factory, to incorporate a display area where visitors can learn about the building and about the lino industry, and to provide prayer and meeting spaces for a local Islamic group. The building's new users could enjoy the sun streaming through the great windows once again.

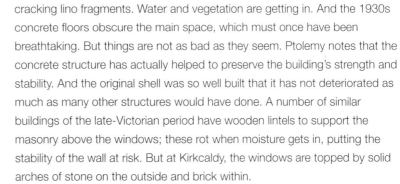

Mavisbank House LOANHEAD

Foundation stone of the Scottish enlightenment

The high quality masonry of Mavisbank's compact central block has stood up well to the tests of time and neglect, even though the roof and many other parts of the structure have gone.

OPPOSITE Curving connecting passages with round-headed windows complement the straight lines of the main house and side wings.

Small, beautifully proportioned, and very fragile, Mavisbank is one of Scotland's most important houses. Ptolemy describes its architecture as being as close to perfection as you can get. Begun in the 1720s by a young baronet and one of Scotland's greatest architects, Mavisbank was one of the buildings that brought the European-influenced classical style to Scotland. It was thus at the forefront of the Scottish enlightenment, the movement that fostered advanced art, science and philosophy, and made Edinburgh into the 'Athens of the North'. It is a major eighteenth-century building, but it has only just managed to survive into the twenty-first century.

Mavisbank House is in the Esk Valley near Loanhead, only a few miles from the centre of Edinburgh. It was built by Sir John Clerk of Penicuik, the cultivated son of a Montrose merchant who had made his fortune trading in Europe. Having studied law at Glasgow and Leiden in the Netherlands, Clerk set off on the Grand Tour through Europe to Italy, where he acquired an extensive knowledge of continental design, spending eighteen months drawing the buildings and antiquities of ancient Rome and reading the classics. He had seen classical buildings throughout Europe and became convinced that this style was the one in which to build himself a new house in Scotland.

By the winter of 1722 he was back home planning just such a house and enlisted William Adam to help him. Adam was a Scottish architect with formidable practical skills and Clerk had a vision of a classical style of building that was new to Scotland; they were ideal partners and together created a gem of a house.

Marianne sums up the building when she says that the design they came up with is grand in style and yet tiny in scale. At the heart is the main house, a compact block only 50 feet by 40 feet. The overall impression of this is classical, with a triangular pediment at the top and pairs of sash windows and a central doorway below, showing the influence of the great Italian architect, Palladio. But the proportions of the windows and the mix of triangular and semi-circular pediments above them, gives the house a Dutch feel. When it was built the whole was topped by a curvaceous roof that was derived from French originals.

The main house is flanked on either side by a pair of smaller wings, linked to the central block by curving corridors, which set it off beautifully, an effect

that is similar to many of Palladio's villas in northern Italy. But again, there are details from other architectural traditions, such as gables in the Dutch style.

It is as if Clerk and Adam were determined to include elements from all over Europe, and to bring as many aspects as possible of advanced European culture to Scotland. Today, the design seems to sum up the educated, enlightened eighteenth century. But in the 1720s in Scotland it was probably quite a shock. For many Protestant Scots, classical buildings like Palladio's were associated with a Catholic culture of which they wanted no part. But this was to change. It was not long before Edinburgh was embracing the enlightenment culture of Europe and classical houses were springing up all over Scotland and beyond. William Adam's sons, John, James, and the famous Robert, were soon spreading the classical style far and wide. So Mavisbank, the first house of its type, has a key place in the history of British architecture.

Scotland added its creative input too, especially in the form of superb craftsmanship. The fine masonry comes straight from the local tradition – the vaulted kitchen passage could almost be in a Scottish castle. But the decoration is much more refined, especially the work of Kirkaldy mason and carver William Silverstyne. Silverstyne carved the fruit, seashells and foliage around the doors and windows, and on the great triangular pediment that tops the façade. Native artists worked inside the house, too. There was rich plasterwork painted by artist James Norrie, some in imitation of marble. At the top of the staircase, a golden plaster sun glinted from the ceiling. This has

BELOW LEFT *Both the fabric and the setting of the house are in urgent need of attention.*

BELOW RIGHT *The elements of classical architecture, such as the triangular pediment and carved cornice, are still visible amongst the dilapidation.*

The tall chimneys and striking gables of the side wings make a strong silhouette.

disappeared, but Ptolemy believes that there is still enough evidence of plasterwork, mouldings and joinery to make a restoration possible.

Despite being such an impressive house it soon fell out of favour. When Clerk died in 1755, his son preferred the family's other, much larger house at Penicuik. Mavisbank passed through various branches of the family, changed hands several times in the nineteenth century, and in the 1880s became a lunatic asylum. But worse was to come. In the 1950s the estate was bought by a new owner, Archie Stevenson, who turned the grounds into a car dump and an unauthorized caravan site. Ptolemy remembers a visit some years ago, when the grounds were a sea of scrap. By that time, the house had also been gutted by a fire, which was probably started deliberately.

Ravaged and unmaintained, it was probably only the quality of the original masonry that stopped Mavisbank from falling down. It is no surprise that in 1987 there was a threat to demolish the house. At the last minute, the local authority secured an order preventing the demolition, mounted a guard, and put up a security fence around the building. Mavisbank was saved – for the time being. Stevenson died in 1993 but played one last trick. He left Mavisbank to three unknown, and probably non-existent, Americans. With ownership in doubt, no restoration took place and the house is still a shell. Scaffolding and bricked-up windows help support the structure, but water and frost damage are doing their worst. The house needs attention, and soon.

So a working group is looking at ways to restore the house and allow public access. A mixed-use scheme is planned, perhaps combining offices and holiday apartments with interpretative displays that explain the history and importance of the house and its role in enlightenment history. Once more, Mavisbank could be an architectural beacon and a focus for the pride of the Scots in their learning and culture.

NORTHERN IRELAND

RESTORATION

Lissan House COOKSTOWN
Herdmans Mill SION MILLS
The Crescent Arts Centre BELFAST

The six counties of Fermanagh, Tyrone, Londonderry, Antrim, Armagh and Down make up the province of Northern Ireland. This is an area with a rich and often troubled history, and a distinctive culture, with buildings that are in many ways quite different from those on the British mainland.

Northern Ireland has some of Europe's most beautiful scenery. The cliffs of the Antrim coast in the north are among the most dramatic in the whole of the United Kingdom. The most famous feature here is the Giant's Causeway, an extraordinary natural formation of basalt rock columns that stretches from the cliffs down to the sea. Another famous sight is the mountains in the southern part of the province, notably the rolling Mountains of Mourne, beloved of walkers.

There is plenty of stone in Northern Ireland. In the Mountains of Mourne it can be seen in the dry-stone walls that divide the fields. In these walls, the rubble-stones are piled haphazardly, often with gaps between them through which one can see the light. The traditional Irish cottage is also built of stone, although many such houses are whitewashed. The simplest design was a single-room farm worker's cottage with stone walls, a clay floor and a roof of either thatch or slates. Such small cottages, extended or subdivided to provide more rooms and more privacy, can be seen in the countryside today. They often stand out, white and isolated, surrounded by the lush green fields where their inhabitants work.

White walls are also common in many town houses. Georgian towns like Hillsborough, south-west of Belfast, have rows of whitewashed or colourwashed houses with slate roofs. A similar delicate colour scheme can be seen in seaside towns such as Portstewart on the northern coast. Here, rows of houses line the seafront, with more rows terraced above and behind them, looking from a distance as if they are built on the roofs of the first.

From very early on, this part of Ireland was a centre of Christianity. St Patrick brought the faith here during the fifth century, and he was followed by other preachers. Soon, Irish monasteries were themselves sending out missionaries, not just across Ireland but also eastwards into Europe. Armagh in particular was an important Christian settlement.

The followers of St Patrick preached the Gospel and founded monasteries in the sixth and seventh centuries. From this time on, monasticism played a key part in Irish Christianity, and monasteries became familiar in the Irish landscape. The ruins of ancient monasteries are scattered over the countryside of Northern Ireland, many of them dating from the tenth or eleventh centuries. Most of these are modest buildings, because the early monastic houses had little money for elaborate church buildings, so the abbeys are usually plain in style, but carefully built.

Often, the most striking feature of an early Irish monastery is a round tower like the one on Devenish Island at the southern tip of Lower Lough Erne. Towers like this are tall and slender, tapering towards a conical roof at the top. Inside, they have wooden floors connected by ladders. First and foremost, round towers were belfries, from which a bell could be rung to call the monks to their regular services. But towers could also act as places of refuge, for monasteries had their fair share of valuables: illuminated manuscripts, jewelled crosses and chalices made of precious metals. The Vikings raided Ireland regularly in the early ninth century, and monasteries were also vulnerable to attack from local lords. A tall tower provided some defence.

Over the centuries many monasteries were extended and new ones were founded, thanks often to support from local rulers. Grey Abbey, south of Newtownards, County Down, for example, was founded by the wife of John de Courcy, one of the knights sent to govern Ireland by the country's first English ruler, Henry II. Begun in 1193, it was the first church in Ireland to be designed in the Gothic style.

But if Ireland was Christian, it was often far from peaceful, with rival Irish kings vying to dominate the land. For much of the early Middle Ages, the area was ruled mainly by members of the Uí Néill family, but different branches of the Uí Néills often warred with one another. Indeed, for much of its history

Whitewashed stone, a slate roof and a tiny porch – buildings like this began life as the simplest of cottages. This one is still fairly simple, although the window in the gable reveals that rooms have been added in the roof space.

Slate roofs and red-bricked mills and houses overlook the River Foyle at Londonderry.

Ireland has been the scene of struggles between rival groups and rulers. The invasions began early, with ninth-century attacks by the Vikings, who later settled in Dublin. The Normans arrived from England in the twelfth century, and the Scots invaded in 1315. More English came later. It is no surprise, therefore, that fortifications, castles and towers soon became an important part of the Irish architectural scene.

One important series of northern castles was put up by the Anglo-Normans in the twelfth century. Carrickfergus Castle, overlooking Belfast Lough in County Antrim, is the most typically Norman, with its great square central tower, with massive walls, very much like the towers that the Normans had built in England at towns such as Rochester and Colchester. The builder of Carrickfergus, John de Courcy, also built castles at Carlingford, Coleraine and Dundrum. The last is perfectly sited on a rocky outcrop by the sea on the coast of County Down. All de Courcy had to do to make the place defensible was to build a wall around the top of the rock. His walls still survive, together with the slightly later round tower in the courtyard, which was added when the castle was owned by King John.

Another style of fortification developed later, in the fifteenth century. This was a time of more stability, when Irish lords and merchants were becoming more prosperous. But they still needed to protect their families and possessions from attack, so they started to build solid-stone tower houses. These were compact, square buildings, several storeys high, with thick walls, small windows and battlements on top. A spiral staircase gave access to the upper floors. Often the tower was surrounded by a yard, called a bawn, which was protected by a stone wall, again topped with battlements. The bawn was an extra line of protection for the tower house and also provided a space where cattle could be kept.

The Irish continued to build tower houses in the sixteenth and seventeenth centuries, and some of the best preserved date from these later years. Narrow Water Castle, north of Warrenpoint, County Down, is an attractive example. Overlooking the approach to Newry harbour, it has stood for almost 450 years and its walls, its vaulted main chamber and its roof are intact.

Tower houses can be bigger and more elaborate than the standard square stone tower. Tully Castle, near Lower Lough Erne, is an example, an early seventeenth-century building laid out like a large capital T. Tully has many of the features of a tower house – it is tall, set within a bawn, has thick walls and most of the windows are quite small – but otherwise it looks more like a conventional house than a tower. It had gabled roofs rather than a flat roof with battlements, although the building is now ruined and the roof covering – which was thatch – has long since disappeared.

Tully Castle dates from the time of James I, when the British Crown tried a new way of controlling Ireland. Instead of relying on military force, as previous rulers had done, James undertook a programme of enforced colonization, known as plantation. Protestants from England were given land in Ireland and built themselves strong houses to protect themselves from attack. Tully is one such 'plantation house'; Monea Castle, north of Enniskillen, County Fermanagh, is another.

By the eighteenth century the Protestant aristocracy of Ireland were doing well and things were more settled. Catholics, by contrast, were not even allowed to buy land. As a result, large Protestant estates developed, and their owners began to build themselves luxurious country houses. They adopted the Palladian style, which was fashionable in England at the time, a style of classical columns, large entrance porticoes and rows of sash windows.

Irish country houses are well known for their interior plasterwork, and one of the best examples in Northern Ireland is Florence Court, near the border to the south of Enniskillen. The original plasterwork was thought to be by a famous Dublin plasterer, Robert West. This work was badly damaged in a fire in 1955, but was replaced from photographs of the original decoration. It is in the flowing rococo style of the mid-eighteenth century.

Castle Coole, south-east of Enniskillen, is one of the finest of Northern Ireland's country houses. It was begun at the end of the eighteenth century, and it is so lavish

Dunluce Castle is set on a 100-foot crag overlooking the sea in County Antrim. A castle was first built on this superb defensible site in the late thirteenth century, but most of the ruins left today date from the sixteenth century.

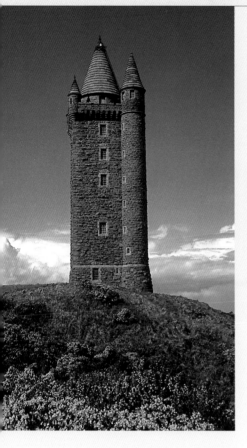

Scrabo Tower, on the Ards Peninsula in County Down, was built as a memorial to the third Marquis of Londonderry in 1857. It is taller and slimmer than a genuine medieval tower house.

that it virtually bankrupted its builder, the first Earl of Belmore. Belmore's son finished the house, decorating it and furnishing it in Regency style in the 1820s. Castle Coole is a three-part house, with imposing façades built of pale Portland stone. In the centre is the main block, with a large entrance portico. Inside are the state rooms, such as the grand dining room and saloon, where the owners did their entertaining. To either side of this block are smaller pavilions, which contain family accommodation and service rooms.

The whole island of Ireland is still known as a mainly rural place, its fields lush and its towns, on the whole, small. But one city did industrialize on a large scale – Belfast. By the eighteenth century, the city had two main industries. The first was linen weaving, which had spread as a result of Huguenot craft workers settling in the city late in the seventeenth century. The other was shipbuilding, with the Harland and Wolf yard eventually growing to a size that could produce one of the greatest ships of all time, the *Titanic*.

Industry brought expansion to Belfast in the Victorian period and the early twentieth century. The shipyards grew, the suburbs expanded and Belfast became the largest city in Northern Ireland – in the whole of Ireland it was second only to Dublin. In addition, Belfast acquired many of the trappings of a major city, with grand buildings that continue to impress visitors today. The public buildings are in a wide range of styles. City Hall, with its tall copper dome, dominates Donegal Square in the centre of Belfast. Its imposing 1906 Renaissance-style exterior houses rooms clad in marble and oak panelling. Queen's University is brick-built in the Tudor manner around a quadrangle. St Anne's Protestant cathedral is imitation-Romanesque, its interior decorated with mosaics. Stormont, the building put up between 1928 and 1932 to house Northern Ireland's Parliament, is in the Palladian style, harking back to the Anglo-Irish country houses. Belfast also has a notable Botanic Garden with a fine iron and glass palm house. Completed in 1853, it has a big glass dome and great curving glass roofs that make it one of the most beautiful of the great Victorian glasshouses.

The Troubles that began in 1968 cast a shadow over Belfast. For a while the city's most famous buildings were houses in the Falls and Shankill Road districts bearing respectively Republican and Loyalist political murals. But the city has entered a period of regeneration. The people are proud of their heritage, and new building schemes are also sources of pride and optimism. One example is the Odyssey complex at Queen's Quay, designed by a local firm, the Consarc Design Group, which combines an indoor arena, an interactive discovery centre, an IMAX cinema and various other leisure facilities. Such ambitious new buildings of today join the renewal of the old to point the way forward to a more positive future.

Lissan House COOKSTOWN

A family home for 400 years

ABOVE LEFT *The curving lines of the porte-cochère were added to Lissan House during the remodelling of 1830.*

ABOVE RIGHT *Tall sash windows flood even the corridors with light.*

OPPOSITE *Nowhere else can there be such a collection of steps, landings and balconies as at Lissan, where the replacement staircase of the 1870s must have been built by a local carpenter who re-used parts of the seventeenth-century original.*

Ireland is famous for its country houses, many of which have been in the same families for many generations. Among these, Lissan House, near Cookstown in County Tyrone, stands out. It has belonged to members of the Staples family for nearly 400 years. But for much of the twentieth century there has been little money for repairs. The current owner, Hazel Radclyffe Dolling, who has looked after the house single-handed for over thirty years, feels that the time has come to rescue the house by giving it a public role that will preserve its integrity.

The story of Lissan House began in the early seventeenth century, when Thomas Staples moved to the estate from nearby Moneymore. Thomas set up an ironworks at Lissan, where a small stone house was already on the site. Thomas's grandson, Robert, rebuilt this house in the late seventeenth century, and traces of his building remain, although many changes were made to the house in the nineteenth century.

Next to the main building is a large courtyard, built on the site of the houses put up by Thomas to house the workers in his ironworks. It now contains arch-fronted carriage sheds, a creamery and other rooms servicing the big house. The walls of the courtyard buildings retain some of their old lime render in what Ptolemy describes as a 'cheesy, creamy colour'. This is a sign of how all the outside walls would have been covered before the fashion for cement rendering in the late nineteenth century.

The house is full of charming spaces with unexpected shapes, like this upper corridor.

Crumbling render provides a major task for the restorer.

The big house itself is cement-rendered now. This and its many sash windows make it look like a nineteenth-century building from the outside. But inside, in the basement, it is possible to find part of the core of the seventeenth-century house in the old kitchen. Massive chimneys, walls six or eight feet thick and ancient oak timbers all point to this early date. These details also reveal that the house was built with local materials. The stone was extracted from a nearby quarry and the bricks were made from clay found on the estate. The Lissan estate also included woodlands, which probably provided the oak beams for what must have been a fine house. A survey of 1703 described it as a 'good stone house' with lofty and large rooms. The accommodation included a handsome hall, a large dining room, a parlour panelled in oak and a good kitchen. The fine staircase leading to roomy accommodation upstairs was also noted.

Much of the rest of the house as it survives today dates from the nineteenth century, from a remodelling that was carried out in around 1830. One of the most striking features of this rebuilding is the entrance porch. This is in the form of a porte-cochère, a large porch into which carriages could be driven. Such porches were fashionable in the early nineteenth century. They were very convenient, especially for well-dressed women who did not want to get their long dresses muddy as they left their carriages. A servant would have been stationed in the porch, warming his hands at the fireplace as he waited for carriages to arrive.

Many of the rooms in the house retain the atmosphere of the early nineteenth-century remodelling, and none more so than the ballroom. This large room retains its neo-classical plasterwork and the beautiful Chinese hand-decorated wallpaper – a rare survival. The windows have small panes of coloured glass around the edges. Several different colours are used, but yellow predominates, and this has the effect of warming the light in the room to give it, in Ptolemy's words, a more Mediterranean quality.

The house was once more improved in around 1870, in the time of Sir Nathaniel Staples. He gave the house a new roof and added the clock tower. Inside, he transformed the staircase to give it the form that can be seen today. This staircase crisscrosses its hall, turning this way and that like a Victorian spaghetti junction as it rises through the house. It passes straight in front of some of the windows in the process, a sure sign that it is not the original. But some of the original components were reused. Seventeenth-century balusters, together with some later Victorian ones in a different wood, support the handrail. No one is sure why the staircase was rebuilt and rerouted in this way, but structural problems, possibly dry rot, probably forced Sir Nathaniel to make the alterations.

So by the beginning of the twentieth century the large four-storey house must have looked very much as it does now, with its pale, rather stark rendered walls relieved by the curving lines of the porte-cochere. The family had one last transformation to make – giving the house an electric power supply. To do this, Lissan was provided with its own hydroelectric system, which still powers the house to this day. The flow of a small stream leading off the lake turns the blades of a turbine, which powers an electrical plant that gives the building its 230-volt supply.

But by the early twentieth century, hit by repeated death duties, the family had little money to make further improvements to the house. Robert Ponsonby Staples, grandfather of the present owner, had to raise money when he inherited the house in 1933, so he sold off most of the nineteenth-century furniture. Staples was known as an eccentric. Nicknamed the 'barefoot baronet', he believed that walking barefoot every day allowed him to absorb life forces directly from the soil. But he was also well educated and had trained as an artist in Europe and exhibited at the Royal Academy. His paintings, however, though widely admired, did not fetch high prices.

The successors of Ponsonby Staples clung on, doing their best to keep the house going. But one person with limited resources cannot maintain a house the size of Lissan. The time has come for the building to be put to a different use, perhaps as a centre for music and the arts, so that many can benefit from it and appreciate its beauties.

The music room – originally the ballroom – is beautifully lit by its generous windows. Large for a domestic room, this space is ideal for concerts featuring small-scale works such as chamber pieces or songs.

Herdmans Mill SION MILLS

Hives of industry by the beautiful River Mourne

ABOVE LEFT *In the shadow of the tall mill chimney some of the lower buildings, with their classical mouldings and pilasters, recall structures of the Renaissance.*

ABOVE RIGHT *This small army of mill works had to negotiate their way through a jungle of belts and shafts that drove the machines.*

OPPOSITE *Iron and steel girders and struts hold up the roof, which was glazed in places to let in plenty of light for the workers.*

Plan for the future – this should be the motto of every business. Herdmans, flax spinners of Sion Mills, near Strabane in County Tyrone, made the maxim their watchword. They provided for the future of their workers, building good housing and a school, running evening classes for the adults and producing enough food on their farms to see them through the potato famine that killed so many in Ireland in the 1840s. And they looked to the future in their business, too. They ensured that their factories had wide interior spaces, so that ever-larger machinery would fit in. And they built solidly, so that their mills could take the relentless pounding as their machinery clattered on through the nineteenth century and into the twentieth.

The business began when the Herdman and Mullholland families bought the Sion complex from the Marquess of Abercorn in 1835. At the heart of the site was a large corn mill, built in 1828 and now known as the Old Mill. Straight away they began to build an additional factory, now called the Main Mill, beside it. Over the years the buildings grew with the business until a huge complex of tall, brick-built structures evolved. It lasted Herdmans until the 1980s, when new technology forced a move to different premises. The mills now stand vast and empty, waiting for conversion to a new use.

At the heart of the complex by the river is the Old Mill, an imposing brick structure enclosing three floors. Each of these is a large, impressive space,

The courtyard contains an extraordinary collection of buildings, of different shapes, sizes and style, some connected together with metal ducting. This variety reveals a site that developed over a long period as the business grew and its needs changed.

OPPOSITE *Much of the original machinery used in the production of linen yarn remains in the mills, making a fascinating record of industrial archaeology.*

with high ceilings and plenty of light from big windows. The huge spaces are uninterrupted apart from slender columns. Up above are vaulted ceilings, and Ptolemy describes how their gently curving brick arches are built to be both strong and fireproof.

The nearby Main Mill is at the centre of the complex today. It was designed by the Belfast architect William Lynn, who started work on the building as soon as the company acquired the site in 1835. Using mainly local sandstone, Lynn designed a very wide building, which proved an excellent investment for the future. Machinery improved as time went by, but it tended to get larger and larger. The Main Mill was big enough to accommodate this new machinery and this ensured its long working life.

As the business prospered, further buildings were added to house extra machines, workshops, maintenance facilities and offices. Most of these extensions were built in yellow brick imported from Kilmarnock in Scotland. It may be that Herdmans chose this material because they wanted to avoid the dark, depressing impression created by most industrial buildings, a notion in keeping with their care for their workers. Certainly there is a feeling of quality about the building. The bricks are well made, and part of the façade curves beautifully. The date lettering is well cut into the masonry, and a tall tower is designed like the campanile of an Italian cathedral.

One part of the complex, the so-called 'New End' of the Main Mill, was built in 1884 and extended upwards with extra storeys in 1907. In this section, the builders eliminated pillars altogether to produce really broad spans of flexible

space. In order to achieve this, the walls were heavily buttressed so that they could support the entire weight of roofs and ceilings. Girders of very heavy section were used so that they did not need to be supported by internal pillars.

The interiors of these buildings are quiet and empty nowadays, and it is difficult to imagine what they would have been like when the mill was working. They would have been noisy places, with the workers straining in an effort to compete with the din of the machinery.

The buildings housed the three different processes used in the production of linen yarn. First there was hackling, a technique used to separate the strands of the flax, rather like carding wool. Then came preparing or drawing the strands into ever-finer fibres. Finally, the flax was spun into finished linen yarn. Flax has to be spun in hot, humid air to keep the fibres supple, so the atmosphere inside the building would have been like a sauna. As Marianne points out, iron grilles in the floor took away excess moisture, and many of the workers paddled around in their bare feet.

The power for all this activity came from the waters of the nearby River Mourne. A section of the river was diverted, and the first water wheels were installed in the late 1830s. Eventually, in the late nineteenth century, the mill began to use electricity, which was generated by the company's own hydroelectric plant. This is still functioning, and now sells its electricity to the National Grid. As a result, water is a vital part of the atmosphere around the mill complex. It flows between the two main buildings, and there is a huge weir and a complicated arrangement of sluices. Not far away, the River Mourne itself provides a picturesque backdrop. In the nineteenth century its beautiful scenery inspired hymn-writer Mrs C. F. Alexander to write 'All Things Bright and Beautiful' in the shadow of the largest linen mill in Ireland.

The builders of the mill did not see a contradiction in constructing a vast industrial complex next to some of Ireland's loveliest landscape. After all, they were at pains to create a pleasant and healthy environment for themselves and their employees. The workers lived in decent housing and enjoyed good health and educational opportunities. There were also recreational facilities, although Herdmans wanted to avoid drunkenness and so for years provided no public house in the village. Most important of all, Protestant and Catholic lived side by side in a generally harmonious atmosphere.

This combination of large, flexible spaces and a good environment is still a strength. The adaptable spaces make it possible to convert the mill buildings for a range of new uses, from flats and workshops to a museum of the linen industry – many similar conversions of industrial buildings in England have shown how successful such schemes can be. The scenery could attract residents and visitors alike, bringing Sion Mills to life once more.

The Crescent Arts Centre BELFAST

A modern use for an old school

The centre's rough-looking sandstone construction is clear on the side elevation, which contains the main entrance.

OPPOSITE *Some of the carved detail around the doorway has worn away, but the slender gothic shaft, topped by a capital carved with 'stiff leaf' decoration, shows the quality of the workmanship.*

This building has been surprising passers-by for 130 years. It is built on to one end of Belfast's only Victorian crescent. The crescent itself is very much as one would expect – a curving line of houses, covered in pale render and picked out with details in the classical style, such as Corinthian columns and pilasters. The building at the end is completely different: of sandstone, it is taller than the adjoining houses and is in a totally different style.

The building, put up as a school in 1873, was commissioned by Margaret Byers, a pioneer of education and one of the few at the time who believed that girls deserved as good a schooling as boys. In 1859 she had started a girls' school, which had proved popular with many moneyed families who would otherwise probably have employed governesses to educate their daughters. Mrs Byers provided a higher standard of girls' education than was usual, more parents flocked to her doors and by 1873 she had borrowed the money to create larger, purpose-built premises.

Margaret Byers chose as architects Young and Mackenzie, a prominent Belfast firm who were responsible for many of the buildings around the City Hall. In the nineteenth century there was much debate about which style was 'correct' or 'appropriate' for which type of building. Many people, for example, thought that Gothic was the only style for churches. For the new school, Young and Mackenzie chose the Scottish baronial style, which is based loosely on medieval Scottish tower houses and castles. Buildings in this style usually have rugged walls and, like castles, are often asymmetrical, and their doorways may have round or pointed arches and other medieval features. The architects probably selected this style because they thought it appropriate for a school.

They created a building with large classrooms on the lower floors, dormitories in the attic and a house for Mrs Byers and her husband, a doctor, to one side. The Ladies' Collegiate School prospered. It was later renamed Victoria College, in honour of the queen, and grew vigorously as Mrs Byers acquired further accommodation in some of the neighbouring houses. The building continued as a school until the 1970s and has housed the Crescent Arts Centre since the 1980s.

The building certainly stands out from its surroundings. Next to the light, elegant crescent, the school looks plain and dark. Its walls have a rough,

Several of the former school's rooms offer spacious settings for all the arts – from dance to painting.

rusticated appearance to give them the rugged air of a Scottish castle. Ptolemy notes that these thick walls were built to last and that they are still giving good service today. Their heavy effect is relieved by several decorative bands of smoother, redder stone at different levels of the building. Tall windows and a roof line broken by dormers complete the picture. From the side, where the building has its main entrance, the impression is different. There is a large, round-fronted bay window, and small stone columns flank the doorway. This entrance front, where parents would enter to meet Mrs Byers, is designed to impress.

The walls of the building are made of soft dark-red sandstone. For the original builders, this had the advantage of coming from nearby Newtownards, so transport costs were low. The sandstone was also easy to work. But although it looks tough, the stone's soft texture is a problem. Close to a railway line, the walls suffered years of smoke pollution, which has blackened the ruddy-brown stone. Worse still, the surfaces are flaking away in many places, posing quite a challenge to the restorer. The solution is probably to remove the flaking pieces and replace them with harder, more durable stone from Scotland. But this would be labour-intensive work with a costly material.

The building was originally in two distinct sections, the house and the school. There are still two staircases: a large one in an open stairwell for the school, and a smaller one, on a more domestic scale, for the house. But otherwise, among the maze of rooms used by the Arts Centre, it is easy to miss the distinction. The larger rooms, though, clearly belonged to the school. The largest of these,

ABOVE LEFT *The Crescent Arts Centre is a victim of graffiti, but many of its rooms have been redecorated to provide clean, white spaces.*

ABOVE RIGHT *Cleanly cut baronial-style detailing is a feature of the exterior.*

the assembly hall, is now used as a dance studio; it has a high ceiling supported by broad beams so that it can be held up without columns. The tall windows let in plenty of light, and the room is still in quite good condition.

Many of the smaller rooms, however, are in a poor state. Half of them are now unusable, and most of the rest may soon become so. In many places, ceilings have fallen in as a result of water penetration. Another challenge is dry rot, which has affected many of the building's timbers. But, as Marianne recognizes, many timbers are surprisingly complete, and there are lots of original features, from the big windows to details such as old doors, corbels and beams. They would be assets in a restored structure. One or two of the rooms have been renovated to show the effect of restoration. With the help of plasterboard and white paint, they have become light, pleasant spaces that are ideal for all sorts of arts-based activities.

Most of the buildings featured in this book stand empty. But the Crescent Arts Centre is well established in the old school and is used by 70,000 people every year. It is the only arts centre in the city that provides classes for ordinary people, young and old, and there is a demand for the extra classes and events that would be possible if all the rooms in the building could be used. Locals have fought hard to save the building before, ensuring the survival of the Crescent Arts Centre through times when it has received very little in the way of funding. So there is no problem with finding a viable use for this building and no lack of vigorous support. The challenge is to raise the money and to make the building safe, accessible and good for another 130 years or more of life at the heart of Northern Ireland's first city.

HOW YOU CAN HELP

Is there a building at risk near you? Are you interested in helping to conserve Britain's buildings for generations to come? The good news is that there are several ways of getting involved and making a positive difference to the country's historic environment.

One possibility is to join one of the groups that campaign for buildings and other aspects of our heritage. Some, such as SAVE Britain's Heritage, work on behalf of a wide range of buildings. Others, such as the Architectural Heritage Fund, can give expert advice to voluntary groups planning restoration projects. They all carry out campaigning work in the widest sense of the word – for example, by educating people about the built environment, running courses, producing publications and posting information on the web. Such organizations are custodians of a rich variety of information, from details of historically correct paint finishes to lists that tell you where the buildings at risk actually are.

If you want to get more deeply involved, you can go further. There are numerous local groups looking after old buildings that rely mainly on help from volunteers – most will welcome enthusiastic helpers with open arms. In many places, people have formed Building Preservations Trusts to restore and preserve historic buildings for the benefit of the public. Organizations such as the Association of Preservation Trusts can give advice. But be warned, this sort of work can take a lot of your time – and can become addictive. You may become so fascinated that you want to go still further, perhaps taking some of the many courses that are available in craft or professional skills. Building conservation can take over your life.

However deep your involvement, though, one thing is clear. Restoring old buildings is a complex, long-term process involving many different skills and even the professionals need the best advice they can get. There are experts in funding, planning, and in every imaginable building craft. So on the following pages you will find a shortlist of key conservation organizations. They are run by some of the best-informed people in the business – and they are enthusiasts too.

Façades with different fates: scaffolding supporting fragile Broomfield House contrasts with the solid walls of Victoria Baths

Ancient Monuments Society

St Anne's Vestry Hall
2 Church Entry
London EC4V 5HB
020 7236 3934

www.ancientmonumentssociety.org.uk

The Ancient Monuments Society was founded in 1924 to foster the study and conservation of ancient monuments, historic buildings and high-quality old craftsmanship. It deals with buildings of all ages and types.

Architectural Heritage Fund (AHF)

Clareville House
26–27 Oxendon Street
London SW1Y 4EL
020 7925 0199

www.ahfund.org.uk

The AHF provides grants, loans and advice to voluntary and community groups involved in restoring old buildings.

Association of Preservation Trusts

Clareville House
26–27 Oxendon Street
London SW1Y 4EL
020 7930 1629

www.heritage.co.uk/bpt

The Association is the membership body for building preservation trusts (BPTs) in the UK. BPTs are charities whose aims include the preservation of historic buildings for the benefit of the public. The association offers members advice and support on running a BPT and doing restoration work.

Cadw

Crown Building
Cathays Park
Cardiff CF1 3NQ
01222 500200

www.cadw.wales.gov.uk

Cadw is part of the National Assembly for Wales. It has a number of responsibilities connected to the built heritage of Wales. These responsibilities include fostering the preservation of historic buildings and ancient monuments, awarding repair and conservation grants, and managing many Welsh ancient monuments.

Civic Trust

17 Carlton House Terrace
London SW1Y 5AW
020 7930 0914

www.civictrust.org.uk

The Civic Trust promotes high standards of architecture and planning in the towns and cities of Britain. It provides advice, technical assistance and other support, makes grants to help people acquire the skills they need to take part in local regeneration projects, and encourages local civic societies around the country. It runs its own urban regeneration unit and campaigns to raise awareness on planning and conservation issues that affect the urban environment.

English Heritage

23 Savile Row
London W1X 1AB
020 7973 3000

www.english-heritage.org.uk

English Heritage advises the government on the historic environment. The organization is sponsored by the Department for Culture, Media and Sport and works with various government departments, local authorities and voluntary bodies to conserve the historic environment, increase people's understanding of the past, and allow public access to England's heritage. Its functions range from awarding grants to caring for ancient monuments. It maintains a Buildings at Risk Register for England.

Historic Scotland

Longmore House
Salisbury Place
Edinburgh EH9 1SH
0131 668 8600

www.historic-scotland.gov.uk

Historic Scotland is an agency within the Education Department of the Scottish Executive. It safeguards Scotland's built heritage and promotes its understanding and enjoyment. It works to improve standards of conservation, awards conservation grants, carries out archaeological programmes and cares for many of Scotland's most important historic buildings.

Institute of Historic Building Conservation (IHBC)

3 Stratford Road
Tunbridge Wells
Kent TN2 4QZ
01747 871717

www.ihbc.org.uk

The IHBC is a professional body representing those working in conservation in both public and private sectors. It aims to set and promote the highest standards in conservation practice.

National Trust
36 Queen Anne's Gate
London SW1H 9AS
0870 609 5380

www.nationaltrust. org.uk

The National Trust is a registered charity, independent of government, and was set up in 1895 to preserve places of historic interest and natural beauty. It now protects more than 250 historic houses and other buildings in England, Wales and Northern Ireland, and opens them to the public, as well as looking after more than 600,000 acres of countryside. The National Trust runs a variety of educational programmes and events. It produces books on conservation and related issues and publishes a magazine covering its work.

National Trust for Scotland
Wemyss House
28 Charlotte Square
Edinburgh EH2 4ET
0131 243 9300

www.nts.org.uk

The National Trust for Scotland is a conservation charity. It works in Scotland in a similar way to its counterpart, the National Trust, caring for and promoting historic buildings, gardens and landscapes.

Royal Institute of British Architects (RIBA)
66 Portland Place
London W1B 1AD
020 7580 5533

www.riba.org

RIBA promotes architecture and fosters excellence in the profession. Its many services include running lectures, events and exhibitions; working in schools and the community; and validating architectural courses both in Britain and overseas. It runs a number of prestigious architectural awards, offers specialist services to its 30,000 members all over the world, and maintains the world's best architectural library.

SAVE Britain's Heritage
77 Cowcross Street
London EC1M 6BP
020 7253 3500

www.savebritainsheritage.org

SAVE was created to campaign for threatened historic buildings. It has lobbied on behalf of buildings of all kinds, has set up charitable trusts to restore threatened buildings and has influenced legislation affecting the built environment. It maintains its own register of threatened historic buildings.

Society for the Protection of Ancient Buildings (SPAB)
37 Spital Square
London E1 6DY
020 7377 1644

www.spab.org.uk

Founded by designer, writer and reformer William Morris in the nineteenth century, SPAB is now the country's largest pressure group fighting to save old buildings from damage and demolition. SPAB trains conservation practitioners, advises owners of old buildings and campaigns on behalf of threatened buildings. The organization also produces publications giving guidance on the care and repair of old buildings.

Scottish Civic Trust
Tobacco Merchant's House
42 Miller Street
Glasgow G1 1DT
0141 221 1466

www.scotnet.co.uk/sct

The Scottish Civic Trust aims to raise the quality of the built environment in Scotland. It works with the planning authorities on proposals that affect the character of listed and other buildings of interest and encourages both the conservation of older buildings and high quality in new construction. It also maintains Scotland's Buildings at Risk Register.

Ulster Architectural Heritage Society
66 Donegall Pass
Belfast BT7 1BU
01232 550213

www.uahs.co.uk

The society campaigns, educates and produces publications. It also collects data on buildings at risk in Northern Ireland.

PLACES TO VISIT

As well as details of whether the Restoration buildings are accessible to the public or not, this list includes some of Britain's most remarkable buildings, including many that are mentioned in this book. But it is just a selection. There are many more included in annual listings publications such as the handbooks produced by the National Trust and English Heritage and Hudson's Historic Houses and Gardens.

Key

EH English Heritage property
EHS Environment and Heritage Service property
HS Historic Scotland property
NT National Trust property
NTS National Trust for Scotland property
Cadw Property in the care of Cadw – Welsh Historic Monuments

Note on opening times

Year-round opening indicates open throughout the year but not necessarily on every day of the week. Enquire about opening times before a visit. Many properties, especially historic houses, are open only one or two days a week. Cathedrals are generally open every day, but visitors should respect service times.

THE SOUTH WEST
Restoration candidates

Poltimore House
Poltimore
Exeter
Devon EX4 0AU

Not accessible to the public although it can be glimpsed from the M5.

Arnos Vale Cemetery
Bath Road
Bristol BS4 3EW

Open to the public during daylight hours.

Whitfield Tabernacle
Park Road
Kingswood
Bristol BS15 1QU

Exterior can be viewed from the street.

Places to visit

Stonehenge
Amesbury
Wiltshire SP4 7DE
01980 624715

Year-round opening

Massive ritual monument, begun around 5,000 years ago and altered over hundreds of years. Stone circles made up of huge rectangular sarsen stones and smaller bluestones. The country's most important prehistoric site. **EH**

Avebury Stone Circles
Avebury
Marlborough
Wiltshire SN8 1RF
01672 539250

Year-round opening

The remains of large prehistoric stone circles completely surrounding the modern village of Avebury. Important museum of prehistory. **EH/NT**

Buckland Abbey
Yelverton
Devon PL20 6EY
01822 853607

Seasonal opening.

House converted from a medieval monastery to create a comfortable Tudor manor house, the home of Sir Francis Drake. Notable Tudor interiors, plus monastic barn.

Arnos Vale Cemetery

Gloucester Docks

Cotehele
St Dominick
Saltash
Cornwall PL12 6TA
01579 351346

Seasonal opening.

Stone-built house built between fifteenth and seventeenth centuries, its charming small rooms have been little altered since. Set in a large estate with gardens and country walks. **NT**

Montacute House
Montacute
Somerset TA15 6XP
01935 823289

Seasonal opening.

Superb Elizabethan house with elaborate chimneys and carvings outside, panelling, plaster ceilings, and ornate chimneypieces within. Rooms include an exceptional long gallery. **NT**

Gloucester Docks
Central Gloucester

Some buildings used as museums, some viewable from outside, Restored area around old docks, with several tall nineteenth-century warehouses adapted for various new uses, including museums, an antiques centre, and offices.

British Empire and Commonwealth Museum
Station Approach
Temple Meads
Bristol BS1 6QH
0117 925 4980

Year-round opening

New museum housed in former GWR station.

Salisbury Cathedral
Bishop's Walk
Salisbury
Wiltshire SP1 2EJ

Year-round opening

Cathedral begun in 1220 and built almost entirely in the early English gothic style. Only the famous spire, Britain's tallest, was added later, in the 1330s.

Wells Cathedral
Cathedral Green
Wells
Somerset BA5 2UE

Year-round opening

Cathedral built and extended throughout the Middle Ages notable especially for its west front, the huge reinforcing arches below the central tower and the vaulted chapter house.

Exeter Cathedral
South Street
Exeter
Devon EX1 1HS

Year-round opening

Cathedral begun by the Normans but remodelled later in the Middle Ages, notable for its beautiful vaulting and the rare surviving sculptures on its west front.

Wells Cathedral

Gloucester Cathedral
Westgate Street
Gloucester GL1 2LR

Year-round opening

Cathedral with fourteenth-century work that is some of the first in the English Perpendicular style.

THE SOUTH EAST
Restoration candidates

Broomfield House
Broomfield Park
Broomfield Lane
Palmers Green
London N13

Not accessible but can be viewed from the public park in which it stands.

Wilton's Music Hall

Wilton's Music Hall
Grace's Alley
Ensign Street
London E1 8JD

Entrance can be viewed from street and the interior is open occasionally for theatrical shows. Call 020 7702 9555 for details.

Darnley Mausoleum
Cobham Park
Kent KT11 3LD

Can be viewed from public park in which it stands.

Places to visit

Fishbourne Roman Palace
Salthill Road
Fishbourne
Chichester
West Sussex PO19 3QR
01243 785859

Year-round opening.

Enormous palace built by a Romanized British leader. The outstanding survivals are the mosaic floors, with their images of mythical beasts such as aquatic horses and sea-panthers.

Weald and Downland Open Air Museum
Singleton
Chichester
West Sussex PO18 0EU
01243 811348

Year-round opening.

Unique collection of more than 40 early buildings, rescued from destruction, moved to the museum site, and restored. Structures include houses, farm buildings, a smithy, a market hall, and a water mill.

Rochester Castle
Rochester-upon-Medway
Kent ME1 1SX
01634 402276

Year-round opening.

Massive stone tower, one of the first castles to be erected by the invading Normans in the eleventh century. **EH**

Bodiam Castle
Bodiam
Robertsbridge
East Sussex TN32 5UA
01580 830436

Year-round opening.

Late fourteenth-century castle built around a courtyard and surrounded by a broad moat. Round towers and many interesting defensive features. **NT**

Hever Castle
Hever
Edenbridge
Kent TN8 7NG
01732 865224

Seasonal opening.

Medieval castle extended during the Tudor period, when it was the family home of Anne Boleyn. Notable gardens, laid out in the early 1900s.

Knole
Sevenoaks
Kent TN15 0RP
01732 462100

Seasonal opening.

England's largest private house, built around several courtyards and little altered since the eighteenth century. Famous collection of furniture, tapestries, and paintings of the seventeenth century. **NT**

The Royal Pavillion, Brighton

Uppark
South Harting
Petersfield
West Sussex GU31 5QR
01730 825415

Seasonal opening.

Superb late-seventeenth-century house with eighteenth-century interiors famously restored after a fire in 1989. Award-winning exhibition tells the story of the restoration. **NT**

The Royal Pavilion
Brighton
East Sussex BN1 1EE
01273 290900

Year-round opening.

Fantasy house created by John Nash for the Prince Regent in 1815–22. Indian-style onion domes combine with Chinese-inspired interiors. Large banqueting room recently restored.

Hampton Court Palace
Hampton Court
Surrey KT8 9AU
020 8781 9500

Year-round opening.

Royal palace built originally in the Tudor period and extended in the seventeenth century by Sir Christopher Wren. Includes vast great hall, lavish state apartments, and large Tudor kitchens.

Windsor Castle
Windsor
Berkshire SL4 1NJ
01753 869898

Year-round opening.

Royal castle begun in the Middle Ages and extended and adapted by many monarchs, especially by George IV in the nineteenth century.

Chiswick House
Burlington Lane
London W4 2RP
020 8995 0508

Year-round opening.

The first of England's Palladian villas, designed for his own use by Lord Burlington in the 1720s, with dome, columned portico, and classical detailing. **EH**

Winchester Cathedral
Winchester
Hampshire SO23 9LS

Year-round opening.

Cathedral with Norman transepts and large nave remodelled in the Perpendicular style to make it the longest of all the country's cathedrals.

Canterbury Cathedral
Canterbury
Kent CT1 2EH

Year-round opening.

Medieval cathedral altered over hundreds of years. Ancient Norman crypt, nave designed by important medieval mason Henry Yevele, and famous shrine of the martyr, St Thomas Becket.

St Paul's Cathedral
St Paul's Churchyard
London EC4M 8AE

Year-round opening.

London's main Anglican cathedral, built by Sir Christopher Wren after its predecessor was destroyed by the Great Fire of London in 1666. Good example of Wren's classical style.

Bateman's Mill
Burwash
East Sussex TN19 7DS
01435 882302

Seasonal opening.

Water mill by the River Dudwell built by an ironmaster in the seventeenth century. Now worked occasionally to grind flour. **NT**

THE MIDLANDS
Restoration candidates

Newman Brothers
Fleet Street Works
Birmingham B3 1JU

Exterior can be viewed from street in Birmingham's famous jewellery quarter.

Arkwright's Mill
Cromford
Derbyshire DE4 3RQ

A heritage site, the grounds of which are open to the public.

Bethesda Chapel
Albion Street
Stoke-on-Trent
Staffordshire ST1 1QL

Exterior can be viewed from the street.

Places to visit

Stokesay Castle
Craven Arms
Shropshire SY7 9AH
01588 672544

Year-round opening.

Well preserved fortified manor house of the thirteenth century. Great hall, large tower, and timber-framed gatehouse make an impressive group. **EH**

Little Moreton Hall
Congelton
Cheshire CW12 4SD
01260 272018

Seasonal opening.

One of the best examples of a timber-framed manor house in England. Early windows and wall paintings, and the top-floor long gallery are outstanding features. **NT**

Burghley House
Stamford
Lincolnshire PE9 3JY
01780 752451

Seasonal opening.

Bethesda Chapel

Little Moreton Hall

Palatial home of William Cecil, Lord Treasurer of Elizabeth I. Interiors richly remodelled in the seventeenth century with wall paintings and carved decoration.

Wollaton Hall
Wollaton Park
Nottingham NG8 2AE
0115 9153900

Year-round opening.

Large Elizabethan 'prodigy house' with tall, tower-like central hall. The building now houses a natural history museum

Hardwick Hall
Doe Lea
Chesterfield
Derbyshire S44 5QJ
01246 850430

Seasonal opening.

Stunning Elizabethan House of Elizabeth Shrewsbury, 'Bess of Hardwick'. Striking exterior and notable interior rooms, including the High Great Chamber, one of the most beautiful rooms of the period. **NT**

Shakespeare Houses
Shakespeare Birthplace Trust
Henley Street
Stratford-upon-Avon
Warwickshire CV37 6QW
01789 204016

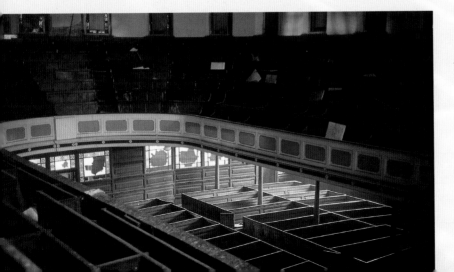

Year-round opening.

Several timber-framed houses in and around Stratford are associated with the dramatist and his family. Shakespeare's Birthplace and Hall's Croft are in the centre of the town; Anne Hathaway's Cottage is at Shottery, just outside Stratford.

Oxford Colleges
Central Oxford

Year-round opening.

Oxford's Colleges include Merton, with its medieval Mob Quad, vast Tudor Christchurch, New College with its fine chapel, and smaller colleges such as Lincoln and Corpus Christi.

Chatsworth
Bakewell
Derbyshire DE45 1PP
01246 582204

Seasonal opening.

Country house of the Dukes of Devonshire, with largely unaltered seventeenth-century state rooms and an art collection, set in a 105-acre park.

Ironbridge Gorge Museums
Ironbridge
Telford
Shropshire TF8 7AW
01952 433522

Year-round opening.

Complex of museums and buildings bringing to life the role of this area in the industrial revolution. Highlights include a recreated Victorian town and the world's earliest iron bridge.

Boulton's Soho House
Soho Avenue
Handsworth
Birmingham B18 5LB

Year-round opening.

Restored eighteenth-century house, the home of Matthew Boulton.

THE EAST
Restoration candidates

Coalhouse Fort
Princess Margaret Road
East Tilbury
Essex RM18 8PB

Open to public at certain times.
Call 01375 385484 for details.

Moulton Windmill
High Street
Moulton
Lincolnshire PE12 6QB

There are occasional tours.
Call 01406 373368 for details.

Greyfriars Tower
Tower Gardens
St James' Street
King's Lynn
Norfolk

Exterior can be viewed from the small park in which it stands.

Places to visit

Hedingham Castle
Castle Hedingham
Halstead
Essex CO9 3DJ
01787 460261

Seasonal opening.

Well preserved Norman keep.

Castle Rising Castle
Castle Rising
King's Lynn
Norfolk PE32 2XD

Year-round opening.

Impressive Norman keep intended originally for the wife of King John. **EH**

Coalhouse Fort

Tatershall Castle
Tatershall
Lincolnshire LN4 4LR
01526 342543

Seasonal opening.

Brick-built tower of the mid-fifteenth century. Restored in the early twentieth century by Lord Curzon, a famous early rescue of an important building. **NT**

Blickling Hall
Blickling
Norwich NR11 6NF
01263 738030

Seasonal opening.

Beautiful Jacobean house set in parkland. Its striking gabled form contains ornate plastered ceilings, and typical rooms of the period, including a long gallery. **NT**

Clare College, Cambridge

Cambridge Colleges
Central Cambridge

Year-round opening.

An architectural feast of a wide range of periods from medieval to modern. Highlights include St John's College with its Tudor gatehouse, Trinity with its Great Court, Clare with its Jacobean and classical features, and King's with its famous fan-vaulted chapel.

Saxtead Green Post Mill
Saxtead Green
Framlingham
Suffolk IP13 9QQ
01728 685789

Seasonal opening.

Large post mill with roundhouse at the base and weatherboarded superstructure or buck. Last worked in the 1940s, the mill's machinery is preserved. **EH**

Bourn Post Mill
Bourn
Cambridgeshire CB3 7SU

Seasonal opening.

Very small mill, with restricted opening, which may be Britain's oldest. Its simple structure gives an idea of what windmills were probably like in the Middle Ages.

Lincoln Cathedral
Lincoln LN2 1PX

Year-round opening.

Arguably the finest of all Britain's cathedrals. Set on a hill, the building's three stately towers can be seen for miles. Inside key features are the gothic nave and the angel choir with its outstanding carved decoration.

Ely Cathedral
Broad Street
Ely
Cambridgeshire CB7 4DL

Year-round opening.

Cathedral famous for its gothic lantern tower, a unique octagonal design.

Norwich Cathedral
The Close
Norwich NR1 4EH

Year-round opening.

Rows of round-headed arches dominate Norwich's Norman nave. The building also has important work of the late-Gothic period, notably fine stone vaults.

Peterborough Cathedral
Minster Precincts
Peterborough
Cambridgeshire PE1 1XS

Year-round opening.

A superb Norman interior, the most perfect apart from Durham. Later additions include the unusual west front with its three deep gothic arches.

THE NORTH WEST
Restoration candidates

Bank Hall
Liverpool Road
Bretherton
Chorley
Lancashire PR26 9AX

Occasional fundraising events are held in the grounds. Go to www.bankhall.org.uk for details.

Brackenhill Tower
Brackenhill Farm
Longtown
Carlisle
Cumbria CA6 5TU

Not accessible to the public.

Victoria Baths
Hathersage Road
Manchester M13 0FE

Tours are held occasionally. Go to www.victoriabaths.org.uk for details.

Places to visit

Carlisle Castle
Carlisle
Cumbria CA3 8UR
01228 591922

Year-round opening.

A fascinating collection of towers, walls, and passages that make up one of our most impressive medieval castles. Reconstructed medieval rooms give an idea of what the living apartments would have been like in the middle ages. **EH**

Penrith Castle
Penrith
Cumbria
0161 242 1400

Year-round opening.

Fourteenth-century sandstone castle built to defend the town from raiders from Scotland. **EH**

Rufford Old Hall
Rufford
Ormskirk
Lancashire L40 1SG
01704 821254

Seasonal opening.

Outstanding sixteenth-century timber-framed house with grand great hall and seventeenth-century brick-built extension. **NT**

Levens Hall
Kendal
Cumbria LA8 0PD
01539 560321

Seasonal opening.

Stone Elizabethan house built around the remains of a medieval tower house. Set in a garden with some famous examples of topiary.

Muncaster Castle
Ravenglass
Cumbria CA18 1RQ
01229 717614

Seasonal opening.

Low-slung battlemented manor house with mullioned windows and tough rubblestone walls.

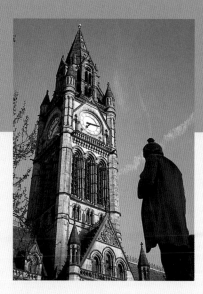

Manchester Town Hall

Manchester Town Hall
Albert Square
Manchester M60 2LA
0161 234 5000

Tours by arrangement; exterior viewable.

One of the great Victorian civic buildings, with a dramatic gothic façade topped by a forest of spires and pinnacles.

Manchester City Art Gallery
Mosley Street
Manchester M2 3JL
0161 235 8888

Year-round opening.

Neo-Classical building designed by Charles Barry.

Liverpool St George's Hall
Lime Street
Liverpool L1 1JJ
0151 707 2391

Events venue; tours by arrangement.

Imposing classical structure with rows of columns that dominate a group of municipal buildings of the mid-to-late nineteenth century.

Albert Dock, Liverpool

Liverpool Walker Art Gallery
The Walker
William Brown Street
Liverpool L3 8EL
0151 478 4199

Year-round opening.

Designed by Cornelius Sherlock, one of Liverpool's collection of civic buildings where the interior is easily accessible to visitors.

Liverpool Albert Dock
Albert Dock
Liverpool

Year-round opening.

Outstanding collection of dockland warehouses restored and converted for new uses as part of a regeneration scheme.

Halifax Piece Hall
The Piece Hall
Halifax HX1 1RE
01422 368725
(Tourist Information Centre)

Year-round opening.

Unique eighteenth-century Italianate courtyard where merchants traded in cloth. A modern market takes place in the large restored courtyard.

Burnley Queen Street Mill
Queen Street Mill
Harle Syke
Burnley
Lancashire BB10 2HX
01282 412555

Seasonal opening.

Nineteenth-century cotton-weaving mill. Several hundred looms are still powered by the steam engine built in 1895.

Port Sunlight
Port Sunlight Heritage Centre
95 Greendale Road
Port Sunlight
Cheshire CH62 4XE
0151 644 4800

Year-round opening.

Unique 'model town' built by soap manufacturer Thomas Lever to house his workers in pleasant, healthy surroundings.

THE NORTH EAST
Restoration candidates

Ravensworth Castle
Cross Lane
Lamesley
Gateshead
Tyne and Wear NE11 9HQ

Not accessible to the public.

Harperley Prisoner-of-War Camp
Harperley
Crook
County Durham

Not accessible to the public.

Wentworth Castle Gardens
Stainborough
South Yorkshire S75 3ET

Occasional gardens tours allow exteriors of both buildings to be viewed. Call 01226 731269 for details.

Places to visit

Chesters Roman Fort
Chollerford
Hexham
Northumberland NE46 4EP
01434 681379

Year-round opening.

Well preserved site of a roman fort near Hadrian's Wall, with bath house and many other buildings. **EH**

Corbridge Roman Site
Corbridge
Northumberland NE45 5NT
01434 632349

Year-round opening.

Remains of Roman town, important military supply depot, and a series of forts near Hadrian's Wall. A museum contains many important finds. **EH**

South Shields Roman Fort
Baring Road
South Shields
Tyne and Wear

Year-round opening.

Interesting remains of Roman fort. A reconstructed gateway gives a good idea of what the building would have been like originally.

Richmond Castle
Richmond
North Yorkshire DL10 4QW
01748 822493

Year-round opening.

Large medieval castle with tall Norman keep affording fine views and a range of domestic buildings dating to the eleventh century. **EH**

The conservatory at Wentworth Castle

Pickering Castle
Pickering
North Yorshire YO18 7AX
01751 474989

Year-round opening.

Walls, keep, and early earthworks survive. The original motte, or mound, survives, where the Normans built their first wooden castle before putting up the stronger stone structures visible today. **EH**

Helmsley Castle
Helmsley
North Yorkshire YO6 5AB
01439 770442

Year-round opening.

Norman keep and outstanding earthworks dominate the centre of this small Yorkshire town. **EH**

Castle Howard
York
North Yorkshire YO60 7DA
01653 648444

Seasonal opening

Grand country house designed by Sir John Vanbrugh and built in the early eighteenth century.

Durham Cathedral
Palace Green
Durham

Year-round opening.

The finest of Britain's Norman cathedrals, Durham stands high above the River Wear. Its striking, deeply carved pillars, round-headed arches, and early stone vault all add to the impression of grandeur.

Richmond Castle

York Minster
York YO1 7HH
01904 557216

Year-round opening.

York is famous for its windows, which preserve some of the finest surviving medieval stained glass.

Rievaulx Abbey
Rievaulx
Helmsley
North Yorkshire YO6 45LB
01439 798228

Year-round opening.

Ruined Cistercian abbey of the twelfth century set in a wooden river valley. The plain gothic arches are typical of the Cistercian style of building. **EH**

Jervaulx Abbey
Ripon
North Yorkshire HG4 4PH
01677 460391

Year-round opening.

Isolated ruins of a medieval abbey, part of Yorkshire's twelfth-century Cistercian boom.

Caernarfon Castle

Byland Abbey
Coxwold
Helmsley
North Yorkshire YO6 4BD
01347 868614

Seasonal opening.

Ruins of Britain's longest Cistercian abbey, with notable rose window and medieval tiles. **EH**

Fountains Abbey
Ripon
North Yorkshire HG4 3DY
01765 608888

Year-round opening.

Britain's best preserved and most striking Cistercian ruins. The walls of the church survive to roof level in some places and the remains of many of the monk's living and working quarters can still be seen. The site has a stunning setting. **NT**

Clifford's Tower
Clifford Street
York YO1 1SA
01904 646940

Year-round opening.

Fortified tower of the thirteenth century in the centre of York. The tower is built on a mound constructed by William the Conqueror as part of his campaign to subdue the city. **EH**

Whitby Abbey and church
Whitby
North Yorkshire YO22 4JT
01947 603568

Year-round opening.

Ruined abbey and medieval church on the edge of the beautiful town of Whitby. The church has outstanding pews, galleries, and pulpit added in the seventeenth and eighteenth centuries. **EH**

WALES
Restoration candidates

Faenol Old Hall
Faenol Estte
Bangor
Gwynedd LL57 4BP

Call 01248 670444 for details.

Amlwch and Parys Mountain
Amlwch
Anglesey LL68 9UT

The port can be accessed at all times and some buildings are open to the public. There are footpaths across the mountain and details of trails can be found at the car park at the top.

Llanelly House
20–24 Vaughan Street
Llanelli
Carmarthenshire SA15 3TY

Exterior can be viewed from the street.

Places to visit

Caerleon Roman Baths and Amphitheatre
5 High Street
Caerleon
Gwent NP6 1AE

Year-round opening.

Remains of fort, barrack blocks, round amphitheatre, and bath complex, plus excellent museum of artefacts found nearby. **Cadw**

Faenol Old Hall

Caernarfon Castle
Castleitch
Caernarfon
Gwynedd LL55 2AY
01286 677617

Year-round opening.

Huge castle built by English king Edward I during his campaigns against the Welsh. Massive walls and polygonal towers shield large courtyards containing royal accommodation. **Cadw**

Conwy Castle
Rosehill Street
Conwy LL32 8AY
01492 592358

Year-round opening.

Outstanding castle of Edward I, with rows of round towers. The castle is connected to the town walls of Conwy to make one of the most impressive medieval fortifications in the world. **Cadw**

Harlech Castle
Castle Square
Gwynedd LL46 2YH
01766 780552

Year-round opening.

Castle built by Edward I with twin concentric walls for added defensive ability. **Cadw**

Beaumaris Castle
Castle Street
Beaumaris
Angelsey
Gwynedd LL57 8AP
01248 810361

Year-round opening.

The Angelsey castle of Edward I, Beaumaris is a beautiful example of concentric defences, surrounded by a moat. **Cadw**

Criccieth Castle
Castle Street
Criccieth
Gwynedd LL52 0DP
01766 522227

Seasonal opening.

Native Welsh-built castle set on a high rock by Cardigan Bay. Its most impressive feature is the huge gatehouse with its pair of round towers. **Cadw**

Erddig
Wrexham
Clywyd LL13 0YT
01978 355314

Seasonal opening.

Eighteenth- and nineteenth-century house. Erddig is especially famous for its unique records and portraits of its servants and the surviving rooms and buildings in which they worked. **NT**

Cardiff Castle
Castle Street
Cardiff CF10 3RB
029 2087 8100

Year-round opening.

Medieval castle restored and partly rebuilt by architect William Burges for the Marquis of Bute in the nineteenth century. Fantastic interiors, with every detail designed by Burges, evoke his Victorian ideas of a range of styles.

St Davids Cathedral
St Davids
Dyfed SA62 6QW
01437 720691

Year-round opening.

The largest cathedral in Wales. It is next to the ruined bishop's palace, built in the thirteenth and fourteenth centuries.

Blaenavon Ironworks
North Street
Blaenavon
Torfaen NP4 9RQ
01495 792615

Seasonal opening.

Eighteenth-century ironworks with casting house and remarkable 'water balance tower', a lifting mechanism powered by the weight of water. Early housing for the iron workers can also be seen on the site.

Dorothea Slate Quarry
Nantlle
Gwynedd

Seasonal opening.

Enormous quarry with surviving building
to accommodate Cornish steam engine.

HIGHLAND SCOTLAND
Restoration candidates

Kinloch Castle
Kinloch
Isle of Rum

This is now open as a youth hostel.
Call 01687 462037 or 462026.

Easthouse Croft
West Burra
Shetland

Exterior can be viewed from the
perimeter fence.

Kinloch Castle

Glen o' Dee Hospital
Banchory
Aberdeenshire AB31 3SA

Not accessible to the public.

Places to visit

Skara Brae
Sandwick
Orkney
01856 841815

Year-round opening.

Unique group of stone-built houses from
the Stone Age, complete with furniture
made of stone. A recent visitor centre
provides information about the site.

Mousa Broch
Isle of Mousa
off Leebooten
Shetland

Year-round opening.

Well preserved Broch (round, tower-like
fortification) of the first or second
century AD.

Eilean Donan Castle
Dornie
Kyle of Lochalsh
Wester
Ross-shire IV40 8DX
01599 555202

Year-round opening.

Thirteenth century tower house in a
stunning lochside setting. Restored
during the 1920s to make it one of the
most evocative of all tower houses.

Glamis Castle
Glamis by Forfar
Angus DD8 1RJ
01307 840393

Seasonal opening.

Extended and turreted tower house of
pinkish sandstone, remodelled in the
seventeenth century. The castle boasts
some fine seventeenth-century interiors.

Crathes Castle
Banchory
Aberdeenshire AB31 3QJ
01330 844525

Seasonal opening.

Attractive sixteenth-century castle,
modelled on a tower house with turrets,
gables, and parapets making a striking
skyline. The castle has notable
decorative features including carved
gargoyles and painted ceilings. **HS**

Easthouse Croft

Torosay Castle
Craignure
Isle of Mull PA65 6AY
01680 812421

Seasonal opening.

Baronial-style house designed by
architect David Bryce and completed in
the 1850s. The large building is set in
beautiful gardens.

Islay Woollen Mill
Bridgend
Isle of Islay
Argyll PA44 7PG
01496 810563

Seasonal opening.

Working mill equipped with a range of
textile-working machinery, much of it
over 100 years old. Highlights include a
slubbing billy, a machine that draws out
the fibres to prepare them for spinning,
and two spinning jennies, similar to those
used during the industrial revolution.

LOWLAND SCOTLAND
Restoration candidates

Britannia Music Hall
113-119 Trongate
Glasgow G1 5HD

Front can be viewed from the street
and the interior is open occasionally.
Go to www.doorsopendays.org.uk
for details.

Nairn's
Kirkcaldy
Fife

Not accessible to the public.

Mavisbank House
Loanhead
Midlothian

Not accessible to the public.

Places to visit

Culross Palace
Culross
Fife KY12 8JH
01383 880359

Seasonal opening.

Late-sixteenth-century palace and
medieval garden form the focus of this
attractive early Scottish town. **NTS**

Edinburgh Castle
Castlehill
Edinburgh EH1 2NG
0131 225 9846

Year-round opening.

Overlooking both the city and the
surrounding countryside, this is the best
known castle in Scotland. As well as
important architectural features such as
the great hall, the castle contains
important relics of Scottish history, such
as the Stone of Destiny. **HS**

St Giles' Cathedral
Royal Mile
Edinburgh EH1 1RE
0131 225 9442

Year-round opening.

Heavily restored but still impressive gothic
cathedral in the centre of the city. The
church where Scotland's reformation
began, under the leadership of John Knox.

Palace of Holyroodhouse
Edinburgh EH8 8DX
0131 556 1096

Year-round opening.

The official Scottish residence of the
British sovereign, the palace was built in
the sixteenth century and remodelled in
the seventeenth. It contains both
apartments of Mary Queen of Scots and
state rooms used by the present ruler.

Falkland Palace
Falkland
Perthshire KY15 7BU
01337 857397

Seasonal opening.

Ruined Renaissance palace, used as a
country residence and hunting lodge by
a number of Scottish rulers. Highlights
include a fine chapel and the old royal
tennis court. **NTS**

Herdmans Mill

Crichton Castle
Pathead
Midlothian
01875 320017

Seasonal opening.

Large ruined castle with Renaissance details including Italianate arches and a façade of stonework dressed to produce a studded or faceted effect. **HS**

Templeton Carpet Factory
62 Templeton Street
Glasgow G40 1DA

Building used for office accommodation; exterior viewable. Unique façade built of a combination of coloured bricks, sandstone, and tiles, to produce the effect of a Venetian palace.

Egyptian Halls
Union Street
84–100 Union Street
Glasgow G1 3QW

Interior not open; exterior viewable.

Industrial building in which Scottish architect Alexander 'Greek' Thomson abandoned the classical style and created a façade built up with Egyptian-style columns.

Glasgow School of Art
167 Renfrew Street
Glasgow G3 6RQ
0141 353 4524

Some rooms open seasonally; rest used by Art School.

Masterpiece of Glasgow architect Charles Rennie Mackintosh using a fusion of traditional Scottish and modern influences to create a highly influential design.

Willow Tea Rooms
217 Sauchiehall Street
Glasgow G2 3EX
0141 332 0521

Year-round opening.

A Mackintosh building recently restored to provide tea rooms, a gallery, and a shop. A rare chance to see an interior designed by this master architect.

Stirling Castle
Castle Wynd
Stirling
County FK8 1EJ
01786 450000

Year-round opening.

Set on a high crag, this dramatic castle controls major routes across Scotland and so was a key stronghold from the Middle Ages to the Renaissance. The huge complex includes Renaissance interiors and eighteenth-century gun platforms. **HS**

NORTHERN IRELAND
Restoration candidates

Lissan House
Cookstown
County Tyrone BT80 9SW

Not open to the public.

Herdmans Mill
11 Mill Avenue
Sion Mills
Strabane
County Tyrone BT82 9HE

Exterior can be viewed.

Crescent Arts Centre
2–4 University Road
Belfast BT7 1NH

Open to the public.

Places to visit

Devenish Island Monastic Site
Devenish Islan
Lower Lough Erne
Enniskillen
County Fermanagh

Year-round opening.

Set on an island in Lower Lough Erne this site features the best example of an Irish round tower dating to the twelfth century. **EHS**

Grey Abbey
Church Street
Greyabbey
Newtownards
County Down

Seasonal opening.

Built by Cistercian monks in the late twelfth century, this was the first Irish church to be built in the gothic style. There are substantial ruins of the church and refectory, plus fragments and foundations of the other buildings. **EHS**

Carrickfergus Castle
Marine Highway
Carrickfergus
County Antrim BT38 7BG

Year-round opening.

Thirteenth-century castle with square keep and curving outer walls. In the seventeenth century the fortifications were altered so that artillery could be fired from within the walls. **EHS**

Dundrum Castle
Dundrum
County Down

Year-round opening.

A round keep dominates this mainly twelfth-century castle on a rocky outcrop by Dundrum Bay. A gatehouse with twin square towers was added in the thirteenth century. **EHS**

Narrow Water Castle
Warrenpoint
County Antrim BT34 3LE

Seasonal opening.

This small tower house consists of a tall rectangular tower surrounded by a lower bawn wall. The setting, by the River Newry, is very attractive. **EHS**

Tully Castle
Lower Lough Erne
County Fermanagh

Seasonal opening.

This building is known as a tower house, but is more house than tower, with gables showing that there was once a pitched roof. Some of the window openings, adding to the impression of domestic comfort. **EHS**

Florence Court
Enniskillen
County Fermanagh BT92 1DB
028 6634 8249

Seasonal opening.

Notable country house built in the mid-eighteenth century and set near the Cuilcagh Mountains. The interiors display beautiful rococo plasterwork. There are also attractive gardens. **NT**

Castle Coole
Enniskillen
County Fermanagh BT74 6JY
028 6632 2690

Seasonal opening.

Notable late-eighteenth-century neo-classical house designed by James Wyatt. The interiors are slightly later, dating from the early-nineteenth-century Regency period. **NT**

The Crescent Arts Centre

Queen's University Belfast
University Road
Belfast BT7 1NN
028 9024 5133

Part open; exterior viewable,

Built in contrasting red and yellow bricks, the main university building was designed by Charles Lanyon and dates from 1849. Its colonnaded quadrangle is similar to an Oxbridge college.

Belfast Botanic Garden
Botanic Avenue
Belfast BT7 1JB

Year-round opening.

This fine botanic garden boasts a Victorian palm house made of cast iron and glass. Its curving walls make it one of the most beautiful of early greenhouses.

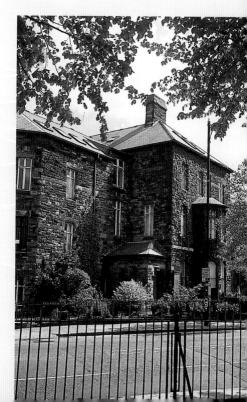

Index